Aristide Maillol
in the 1890s

Studies in the Fine Arts
The Avant-Garde, No. 30

Stephen C. Foster, Series Editor

Associate Professor of Art History
University of Iowa

Other Titles in This Series

Aristide Maillol
in the 1890s

by
Wendy Slatkin

UMI RESEARCH PRESS
Ann Arbor, Michigan

3/84 ꞇꞃᴀꞅ ''

Produced and distributed by
UMI Research Press
an imprint of
University Microfilms International
Ann Arbor, Michigan 48106

Library of Congress Cataloging in Publication Data

Slatkin, Wendy.
   Aristide Maillol in the 1890s.

   (Studies in the fine arts. The avant-garde ; no. 30)
   "A revision of the author's thesis, University of
Pennsylvania, 1976"–T.p. verso.
   Bibliography: p.
   Includes index.
   1. Maillol, Aristide, 1861-1944. I. Title. II. Series.

N6853.M16S57 1982   709'.2'4   82-4799
ISBN 0-8357-1333-4   AACR2

Contents

List of Figures

Acknowledgments

It would have been impossible even to attempt a study of Maillol's early career without the permission of Mme. Dina Vierny. That I was permitted virtually unlimited access to the paintings and statuettes in her extensive collection greatly facilitated my research. Her enthusiasm and wholehearted support for my work has constantly inspired me.

I gratefully acknowledge the substantial contribution of Dr. John McCoubrey, whose intelligent and well-taken criticism of an earlier version has, to a large extent, determined the final form of this work. I feel myself very fortunate to have had the opportunity to benefit from his scholarship and his visual sensitivity.

I would also like to thank Mr. John Rewald who encouraged me to pursue this topic and shared his personal knowledge of Maillol. He patiently answered my questions and opened the contents of his extensive personal library to me.

Dr. Paul Watson read this text and offered many valuable suggestions which I have gratefully incorporated into this book.

The following persons offered their expertise on specific problems which arose during the course of my research: Mme. Geneviève Souchal, M. Guicheteau, Dr. Paul Watson, Dr. Kathy Hiesinger, and Ms. L. Clarice Davis.

The following private owners most kindly allowed me to view and photograph works in their possession: Mr. Samuel Josefowitz, M. Dominique Denis, M. Bernard-Fort, M. Daniel Guerin, Mme. Gaston Jacquart, Mme. Michel Ranson and Mme. Littaye-Belle. Many of these people knew Maillol and shared their memories as well as their objects with me.

The Petit Palais and Musée National d'Art Moderne allowed me to view Maillol's paintings in their collections. Photographs were provided by La Réunion des Musées Nationaux, Paris; the Museum of Decorative Arts, Copenhagen; and the Museum of Art, University of Kansas, Lawrence Kansas. I would also like to thank M. René Rousseil, who arranged for the photographic documentation of the mural cycle in Banyuls.

Mr. Laurence Alloway provided friendship, guidance and moral support at a crucial stage, for which I am deeply grateful. Dr. Barbara Novak's inspired, electric teaching at Barnard College opened the world of art history to me.

Inexpressible gratitude is owed my mother and father. Their unshakeable faith and moral and financial support sustained me through the years of my graduate education and, indeed, my entire life.

Finally, I want to thank my husband, Michael Katze, who accompanied me to Paris and served as photographer, friend, and confidant while this work was in preparation. I am deeply grateful for his devotion, love, patience, and generosity.

Introduction

This study is focused exclusively upon the works of art—paintings, tapestries and sculpture—created before 1900 by Aristide Maillol (1861-1944). Maillol's reputation in the history of art is based primarily upon a group of large-scaled, i.e., life-sized or larger, bronze and marble statues of female figures, created between 1905 and the year of his death. Maillol did not become a full-time sculptor until he was nearly forty years old, however. He was trained as a painter, and during the 1890s he painted a group of largely unknown and unpublished works. The majority of these paintings rèmained in the artist's possession, and today are in the collection of Mme. Dina Vierny, Maillol's model and companion of his late years. Since Maillol's death, Mme. Vierny has been the devoted guardian of his oeuvre and reputation. An analysis of this early period in Maillol's career would have been impossible without extended access to the Vierny Collection, which was most generously and graciously permitted the author.

The 1890s have generally been viewed as an aberrant period for Maillol; his activity as a painter and tapestry-maker is thought to have held no significance for the artist when he began to create sculpture. This attitude is reflected in the fairly large body of critical literature on Maillol. With few exceptions, all writing has been focused on the sculpture created after 1900. Only one scholarly article is devoted to Maillol's paintings;[1] his tapestries have been included in a survey of European tapestries of the 1890s, with accompanying illustrations.[2] There has been no analysis, comprehensive or otherwise, of Maillol's creations from this early period.

In fact, the years from 1890-1900 comprised the most important formative decade for Maillol's artistic sensibility. During this time, he absorbed a variety of influences, experimented with a number of media, and developed a stylistic and theoretical basis for his art which would serve as the foundation for his subsequent oeuvre. Maillol's two-dimensional works from the 1890s are an absolutely essential portion of the artist's oeuvre, the tangible manifestation of many years of effort and discovery.

This decade in Maillol's life was also significant for his career because the avant garde associations he established had a lasting impact on his stylistic development and his theoretical stance. By the mid-1890s, Maillol was associated with a group of artists known as the Nabis. He developed a close personal and professional friendship with Maurice Denis, the spokesman and theoretician of the group . His relationship with Denis, more than the other Nabi artists, was to be particularly decisive for his career.

In the early 1890s, Denis and Serusier had evolved a Symbolist theoretical position which was clearly neo-platonic. In this respect they were following the trend already established in French literary circles. Jean Moreas's "Manifesto of Symbolism," published in 1886, launched this Idealist movement.[3] After 1898 Denis, in contact with André Gide, identified the art of his time to be based on a French form of classicism. This development from symbolism to neo-classicism was the theme of Denis's first set of collected essays subtitled: "From Symbolism and Gauguin toward the New Classical Order." Maillol's stylistic development in the later 1890s parallels this movement from Nabi-styled symbolism toward classicism.

This avant garde movement grew in influence especially after 1901 with the publication of the journal *L'Occident,* edited by Adrien Mithouard. *L'Occident* was founded to proselytize for a French classicism in all the arts. According to Mithouard, one could detect a classical restraint and simplicity uniting French works of art in all media from many epochs since the Middle Ages.[4] It is within this milieu that Maillol developed his definitive classical style after the late 1890s. It is not coincidental that one of the most important essays on Maillol, written by Denis, was first published in *L'Occident.*[5] While a full discussion of Maillol's relationship with this neo-classical movement is outside the limits of this discussion, it is important to note that Maillol's development toward a purified classicism, which occurred around 1900, was the logical outgrowth of the artistic associations he made in the 1890s.

My research, therefore, was undertaken to reconstruct a crucial and formative creative period of a great artist's career and thereby to define the nature of the foundation upon which the later sculpture was erected. To that end, the full range of Maillol's artistic activity around 1900 has been reconstructed. Maillol's surviving works in each medium have been collected, organized chronologically wherever possible, and analyzed stylistically. Although the greatest attention has been focused on the paintings, this investigation includes tapestries, sculpture in wood and clay, both relief and free-standing, and woodcuts and lithographs.

Maillol often worked in more than one medium simultaneously, particularly after 1895. He frequently transferred a motif from one material to another, modifying the image in the process, thus creating a new work of art. Maillol conceived of himself as a craftsman, and saw no reason to specialize or limit his activities to any single medium. This attitude is not unusual in the milieu of the 1890s. It had been most recently revived by the Arts and Crafts movement in England, and harks back to the Renaissance conception of the artist. This versatility is particularly evident in Maillol's activities in the 1890s, but does continue throughout his life. After 1905, although he devoted most of his energies to sculpture, he still produced graphics. After 1930, he took up painting again, as well. Therefore, it has been impossible to limit this study to any one aspect of his production.

This book begins with a brief biographical sketch which provides an overview of Maillol's life from 1865-1905. Separate chapters are devoted to the paintings, tapestries, and the early small-scaled sculpture. In the epilogue, some connections between the large sculpture and the works from the 1890s are indicated. Amended to the text is a *catalogue raisonné* of Maillol's tapestries.

Although, many of the surviving paintings are beautiful and some are even impressive, Maillol's paintings occupy an admittedly less significant historical position than contemporary works by Gauguin, Denis, or even Serusier, for example. Maillol's tapestries, on the other hand, are among the very finest works created in that medium during this epoch and are fully worthy of formal and iconographic analysis.

However, a detailed examination of Maillol's works, regardless of their intrinsic aesthetic quality, is justified for several reasons. Such an analysis provides not only needed information about this formative decade of Maillol's career, but also an example of the way in which a young, talented artist at this point in the history of art responded to contemporary avant-garde painting. The 1890s were one of the most vital periods of experimentation in the history of modern painting. During this decade artists of both generations, Impressionists and Postimpressionists alike, were reacting in a variety of ways to the impact of Impressionism. The way in which Maillol incorporated and assimilated contemporary developments in the art world provides insight into the way in which one artist "influences" another as well as the way one movement is supplanted by the next.

Recent scholarship has emphasized the fact that any epoch in the history of art is more complex than the accounts of the personal development of a handful of individual geniuses. The history of Postimpressionism, as codified by John Rewald in his monumental and invaluable *Post-Impressionism: From Van Gogh to Gauguin,* deals mainly with Seurat, Gauguin, and Van Gogh. The Nabis are treated rather superficially, and Maillol's paintings and tapestries are barely mentioned. Furthermore, Postimpressionism has been typically viewed as a phenomenon confined to France. By contrast, the recent major exhibition *Post-Impressionism: Cross-Currents in European Painting* reevaluates this era in a much more inclusive manner.[6] Not only were many French artists included in the exhibition who are not generally associated with the movement, but also artists from most major European countries are placed within the context of Postimpressionism. An account of Maillol's development in the 1890s, therefore, is a contribution towards a more complete and more accurate understanding of this extremely complex era in the history of art.

We do not possess a body of original statements by Maillol. From all accounts, he was not a man who expressed his ideas on art freely either in writing or in conversations. In the last year of his life, he was asked to write a statement for a magazine, published near Banyuls, which begins with a negation of the validity of any written explanation of his art: "If you had asked a great musician to tell you what he thought of his music, he would have responded: 'Listen to my works.' My métier is sculpture, my tool is the chisel, I can only express myself with my tool."[7] During his lifetime, he rarely deviated from this dictum.

Our primary knowledge of this artist, therefore, comes from the writings of those who knew him. However, the earliest published pieces about him date from 1905. The information we do possess concerning the first forty years of his life was only recorded much later. The most extensive and reliable biography was written by Judith Cladel, in 1937.[8] A series of articles and a monograph by John Rewald, based on personal encounters with the artist, provides further valuable information. Another primary source for the early career of Maillol is the diary of Dr. Bassères, a childhood friend.[9] A considerably less reliable source for Maillol's statements on his art is Henri Frère's *Conversations avec Maillol.* Although this does provide some valuable insights into Maillol's beliefs and behavior, more often the author's own personality and opinions on art seem to overwhelm his subject.

Significant analyses of Maillol's sculpture began with two extensive articles, published in 1905. Maurice Denis's essay remains to this day one of the most perceptive, sensitive analyses of Maillol's talent.[10] Octave Mirbeau, an influential critic and author of the period, wrote an essay which traced Maillol's development from his beginnings as a painter, through his ceramic work, to his sculpture.[11] Both of these articles were crucial in popularizing Maillol's talents and informing the critical and general public about the, then, virtually unknown artist. These two essays initiate the series of about twenty monographs and over one hundred articles devoted exclusively to Maillol: his sculpture, drawings and book illustrations. The most recent monograph by Waldemar-George is not a scholarly assessment of Maillol's oeuvre.[12] Marcel Guerin published an authoritative *catalogue raisonné* of the graphic works.[13] A *catalogue raisonné* of Maillol's sculpture is in preparation by Mme. Dina Vierny.

Many of the articles are simply descriptions of Maillol's large-scale sculpture. More serious essays attempting to explain Maillol's sculpture generally fall into several broad categories. Certain authors view his statues as a "modern" version of Greek sculpture. Maillol then becomes the latest in a series of interpretors of the classical tradition. Other writers have criticized him for a lack of idealization. In this school, the statues are seen as "mere" copies of the peasant women of Banyuls, his hometown on the Mediterranean. Both views express doubts as to Maillol's creative contribution to his works: Maillol is cast in the role of slavishly copying classical prototypes in the first group, and nature, in the second. (These two views had already been current by 1905, when Mirbeau cites them to explain why Maillol did not receive the commission for the *Monument à Zola* which was given to Constantin Meunier in 1903.) The majority of writers, furthermore, view Maillol's sculpture as the "logical" reaction to Rodin's works. They contrast, formally, Maillol's simplified planes and contours to Rodin's agitated forms. In this school of what one could term "historical determinists," Maillol had no choice, given the point in the history of sculpture when he emerged, but to find a form which was diametrically opposed to that of Rodin.

Maillol's reputation continues to suffer from comparisons with the admittedly more fertile genius of Rodin. Scholarship on Rodin has been active through the 1970s, culminating in the exhibition catalogue *Rodin Rediscovered* (Albert Elsen, editor, Washington D.C. National Gallery of Art, 1981). By contrast, the catalogues of the major Maillol exhibitions in New York (1975), Baden-Baden (1978) and Perpignan and Barcelona (1979) do not contain significant scholarly contributions on Maillol's sculpture.

This situation in art historical scholarship should not be viewed as a reflection of Maillol's historical position. Maillol is the next major sculptor in France after Rodin. Rodin, himself, admired Maillol's early sculpture. *The Mediterranean (La Méditerranée),* exhibited in 1905 had a profound and pervasive impact on many artists, such as Duchamp-Villon, Lehmbruck and Matisse. *The Mediterranean* anticipates the increased impersonality and psychological detachment of early modern sculpture.[14] Furthermore the formal innovations of this sculpture, i.e. its synthetic surface, is of crucial importance for the development of pre-World War I avant garde sculpture.[15]

Although Maillol's most important innovations for the history of sculpture occurred after the 1890s, thus falling outside the focus of this study, detailed attention to this artists's early works is justified because of the importance of Maillol's oeuvre for the history of twentieth-century sculpture. The author hopes that this analysis will expand the body of knowledge about Maillol and aid all who are interested in understanding his contribution to the history of art.

1

A Biographical Sketch: 1861-1905

There is little concrete biographical information concerning Maillol's life from 1861 to 1905. Thus, when one begins to reconstruct the artist's actollections as recorded by Judith Cladel[1] and the diary of François Bassères, a doctor, born in Banyuls-sur-Mer, Maillol's hometown.[2] There are also scattered letters which have survived from this era. The following account integrates all primary sources into a chronologically organized narrative. This is a necessary preliminary task before one can trace Maillol's artistic development. Certain subjects, such as Maillol's relationship with Gauguin, will be discussed in greater detail in subsequent chapters, in relation to specific works of art.

Maillol was born on December 8, 1861, in Banyuls-sur-Mer, then a small fishing village. Banyuls is located fifteen kilometers from the Spanish border on the Mediterranean coast, in that mixed French-Spanish province known as Catalonia. He was the third of four children: Raphael and Marie were born before him and Elisa after him. We know virtually nothing about his mother. His father was a fisherman who was absent for long periods. Perhaps his mother was an invalid because the young boy was raised by two maiden aunts, Lucie and Claire. They lived in a pink house rising on a hillside overlooking the bay of Banyuls; this house was to be Maillol's residence for the rest of his life.

He attended the public school of Banyuls, L'Ecole communale, until he was twelve years old. It was in this elementary school that he met François Bassères who has left us the following description of Maillol as a very young boy:

> I see at the second desk,...almost under the eyes of the teacher, Maillol, a small schoolboy dreamer, or bent over a paper on which he scrawls drawings. I see him only in this attitude of a student dreamer or one who is drawing; already at that time I admired him. "I loved horses and boats," he recalled one day, à propos of these distant memories. I remember it as if it was quite recent. And, to tell the truth, I only remember, in a precise way, these drawings....
>
> Rarely, on leaving school did he join in our games. If Maillol was timid, it was no doubt due to the influence of Aunt Lucie....

We shared a taste for insects. . . . How many victims enriched the scenes of our passionate hunts. Sometimes our schoolboy excursions brought us to the farm. What delightful days we passed there, by the little stream. . . . [3]

Already one can note an interest in the botanical phenomena of the region. This fascination with nature would remain with him as a constant source of joy for the rest of his life. Also, Bassères identifies several personality traits which are consistent with the adult Maillol. Both his shyness, a reserve bordering on the taciturn, and a sense of isolation were already present in the young child, as well as a love for drawing.

Between 1873 and 1878, Maillol pursued a classical education at the lycée, the *collège libre* of Perpignan. In 1874, at age thirteen, he made his first painting, a seascape, *Le Cap d'Ouve*.[4] We know practically nothing of Maillol's opinions and impressions of these six years of schooling. By the time he had completed his course of study at the *collège libre,* he was already set upon becoming an artist. His drawing teacher, a Pole named Alchimovitch, had become curator of the Museum in Perpignan. Maillol was given 200 francs a year by the commune of Banyuls to travel to Perpignan to study with his former teacher. The man agreed to teach him drawing for twenty-five francs a month.[5] His first directive to the young artist was to copy skulls. Frustrated by this strict academic regimen, Maillol ceased paying the monthly fee and decided to work at the museum on his own. While he was drawing there, he met a young Parisian sculptor who was a student at the Ecole des Beaux-Arts. This student's name has not come down to us. He is referred to as "S . . . " in Dr. Bassères's chronicle. The young artist from Paris must have seemed very exotic and worldly to Maillol, who had not been more than fifteen miles away from his birthplace. Always eager to learn, Maillol asked him for guidance in the art of sculpture. The young man said, "Make a foot!" Maillol then proceeded to draw the outline of a foot on a piece of wood and build up the structure in clay, maintaining a hollow interior, as if he were modeling a pot. This direct primitive method of sculpting without an armature apparently surprised the student, used to more sophisticated techniques. When Maillol recounted this story to Cladel, he admitted that he had used a similar technique to model several of his large figures.[6]

Years later Maillol described this young artist to Bassères in the following way:

He was a boy with magnificent eyes. Without a doubt, because of these eyes, I believed he was intelligent. But appearances can be deceptive. . . . However, I worked for several days with S . . . in a small rotunda, behind the large gallery of the Museum, with the willingness of an employee who opened the doors. But the noise of the chisels working the stone, provoked complaints and we had to pack up.[7]

One may assume this contact further solidified Maillol's resolve to travel to Paris and study at the Ecole des Beaux-Arts.

During this three-year period between his graduation from the lycée and his arrival in Paris in November 1882, Maillol illustrated his own periodical. Friends provided the articles for *La Figue,* the title of this "petit revue," but, unfortunately none of the issues have survived.

Upon his arrival in Paris, he moved into the Rue des Vertues, in the area of the Musée des Arts et Metiers. He chose this part of the city because acquaintances from Banyuls were now living there. Maillol felt a very strong identification with his native area of France and throughout his life sought out people from Roussillon as friends.

Upon his arrival, he went directly to the Ecole des Beaux-Arts and began attending the drawing classes of Gérôme (one of the most popular and respected academic painters of the period) as an "élève libre," i.e., a student who has not passed the entrance examinations, and is therefore not officially enrolled. He was extremely poor; he had a living stipend from Banyuls of 200 francs a year. This forced him to live on ten sous a day, "two sous for bread, eight sous for cheese."[8]

After three months at the Ecole des Beaux-Arts, in the above-described status, he showed his drawings to Gérôme. Bassères has recorded this incident, as Maillol described it to him:

> I trembled like a leaf. An urge to turn away seized me. Then, abruptly, I decided... Knock, Knock.—"Enter," cried a terrible voice. I entered... The master, lying flat on the floor before a canvas, was painting. At the sight of this intruder, he stood up. His gaze overwhelmed me, I was frozen. "What do you want, Monsieur?" I told him the aim of my visit. "Very well, Monsieur, show me your drawings." I showed them to him; one glance... and my fate was sealed:—"You know nothing, Monsieur, you may leave. But I want to give you some useful advice: Go and draw at the [School of] Decorative Arts."[9]

This account agrees with that recorded in Cladel. However, when Maillol told Cladel the story, he remembered Gérôme's comment as "You know nothing! Go to the School of Decorative Arts; make noses and ears...."[10]

Gérôme's rejection of Maillol's work did not necessarily indicate that Maillol was lacking artistic talent. A young and aspiring artist was required to pass a very strict entrance exam to enter the Ecole des Beaux-Arts. Maillol, fresh from the provinces and lacking professional training, would surely have failed the test. In order to acquire that training, Maillol followed Gérôme's directive and enrolled in the less restrictive Ecole des Arts Décoratifs. On January 16, 1883, he entered the Sculpture section "for the study of the figure and ornament", under the supervision of Cabanel.

Cladel records the following comments made by Maillol's professors, during his first trimester at the Ecole des Arts Décoratifs:

"Very good student, very intelligent"; "Good student, very steady." The director of the Ecole wrote: "The survey of the notes of the professors and supervisors confirm the good opinion I have of this student. He is assiduous, steady and a hard worker. His conduct is excellent."[11]

However, during his second trimester, he was repeatedly absent from classes and the Director noted that "he must at least explain the cause for his absences."[12] According to Maillol's explanation to Cladel, the late hours, the long walks to and from school, and ill health interfered with his study at this time.

In 1885, Maillol passed his entrance examination at the Ecole des Beaux-Arts. Records preserved in the Archives nationals in Paris show that he was ranked seventy-fourth out of the eighty students admitted.[13] Maillol enrolled in Cabanel's drawing class at the Ecole des Beaux-Arts. Apparently, he was satisfied with Cabanel's instruction and later in life told Bassères, "I have never forgotten the Master [Cabanel] who was very good for me.... I never had any others [teachers] and I remained his pupil for five years."[14]

It must be remembered that a young artist in Paris is influenced not only by his teachers and his classes at the Academy, but also by his friends. Therefore, it is informative to know Maillol's most immediate personal contacts in order to fill in this picture of his Parisian artistic education.

For example, when Maillol was at the Ecole des Arts Décoratifs, he had taken a course in drawing the nude model, under the supervision of Adolphe Yvon. It was in this class that he met Achille Laugé, who was to become a very close friend. Maillol said of Laugé, "It was Laugé who set me on the route."[15] Through Laugé, he met Antoine Bourdelle who was also to become an intimate colleague. In the autumn of 1885, following his acceptance into the Ecole des Beaux-Arts in January of that year, the two friends, Maillol and Laugé both enrolled in Cabanel's painting class. Maillol shared a studio with Laugé for three years (1885 to 1888) and described his artistic activities at this time as follows: "We painted still lives, mainly of apples ... I painted more apples than Cézanne, without ever having seen a Cézanne.... It was the Age of the Apple. It was the epoch when we wasted our time."[16] During this period of study at the Ecole des Beaux-Arts Maillol described Laugé, Bourdelle and himself as "inseparables."[17] But this close friendship only lasted a few years. Once Maillol left the Ecole des Beaux-Arts, he broke off all contact with Laugé.[18] Maillol remained friendly with Bourdelle for several years longer, but when Maillol began to make sculpture, i.e. around 1897, his friendship with Bourdelle, then working in Rodin's atelier also terminated.[19] Later on in his life Maillol said of these two men: "When I began to see what was art, I ended by leaving my comrades because they remained behind. I followed my taste ... I was very independent...."

Maillol also became friendly with the painter Georges-Daniel de Monfreid, in 1882 or 1883. Considering Maillol's intense love for his homeland, the fact that Monfreid was also from Roussillon surely was a factor which bound the two in friendship. Between 1884 and 1897, Monfreid kept a journal of his activities in which he records virtually daily contacts with Maillol both in Paris and in Roussillon.[21] In addition to the evidence from Monfreid's journal, documentary evidence of their friendship exists in the form of drawings in the Monfreid collection.[22]

It was certainly Monfreid who introduced Maillol to Gauguin, probably during the winter months of 1889, when Gauguin was living in Paris. We do not know how often the two met, but we know that a true friendship never materialized between them.[23] Maillol stated this in a letter to Maurice Denis written to thank Denis for his article, in 1905: "Chance had me meet Gauguin before you, but with him friendship was not possible."[24]

In 1889, after five years of study with Cabanel, Maillol left the Academy completely disillusioned with formal instruction:

> I had not learned to draw or furthermore, to paint. Badly taught, or not taught at all, we understood nothing of art.... We were swimming all alone in the stupidity and ignorance which ruled the courses everywhere... Of my colleagues who graduated, not a one became an artist.... [25]

Maillol further criticized the conservative nature of academic painting and instruction: "The Academy rejected the modern movement; however, it liked Puvis well enough, all the while maintaining that he did not know how to draw... Human stupidity is unfathomable."[26] At another point he says, "The unfortunate one falls into the Ecole like into a well."[27]

From his own assessment, Maillol was no more certain of his personal style in 1889 than he had been upon arriving in Paris fresh from the provinces at age twenty-one. This complete absence of a personal style is proven by the fact that the only works which we can date before 1889 are closely imitative of the styles of other masters: such as Puvis de Chavannes and Courbet.

One cannot be absolutely precise in determining a date when Maillol first saw Gauguin's paintings, but it was surely not later than June 1889, when the *Exposition des peintures impressionistes et synthétistes* opened at the Café Volpini, just outside the grounds of the Exposition Universelle. The works exhibited at the Café Volpini, were a revelation to him[28] and one can observe the strong influence of Gauguin on a group of Maillol's paintings from this time. Although this derivative period passed quickly, Maillol did not forget Gauguin's works and continued sporadically to draw inspiration from his paintings during the 1890s and early 1900s.

Despite the fact that Maillol had been attracted to sculpture in Banyuls and had studied sculpture at the Ecole des Arts Décoratifs, his creative energies were focused exclusively upon painting from 1890 to 1893. During these years, he created a series of interesting and beautiful works. Looking back upon this period of experimentation in painting, Maillol viewed it as a time when he struggled to achieve a personal style, searching for that which Denis and Gauguin had already found.[29]

Throughout this era, Maillol was extremely poor. He was not receiving any money from his family or the town of Banyuls and he could not find enough buyers for his paintings. He partially supported himself during the early 1890s by picking up odd jobs when he could find them. One such job was painting theater sets. He told Cladel that he painted a set for Maurice Bouchor's *Petit Théâtre des Marionnettes*. This theater was in operation from 1889 to 1894. *Le Petit Théâtre* performed symbolist favorites, such as Maeterlinck's *Les Sept Princesses;* classics in translation, such as Shakespeare's *Tempest;* and several plays written by Bouchor himself.[30] Maillol remembered that the scenery for *La Dévotion à St. André,* which must have been painted around 1892, was well received:

> When the curtain rose on this one, a large and handsome older man, seated in the orchestra, did not fail to applaud: this was Puvis de Chavannes. Maurice Bouchor, who knew him, introduced him to Maillol: complimented, invited to come to the studio of the famous painter, the artist "too timid, too stupid," never dared to go.[31]

Monfreid also recorded in his diary: "Saw Maillol on my way home, as he left the marionnettes."[32]

We possess another account of Maillol's mural painting commissions during these early years in Paris. Count Kessler, who was to become Maillol's single most constant and generous patron later on, recorded this statement of Maillol's:

> "It was at the Ambassadors where I made my first decoration, on my arrival in Paris. Yes, I decorated the Ambassadors." He was then, without a sou and friends had arranged this job so that he could earn a little money. Finally, he was the only one who was paid, because the administration was thrown out for total incompetence and he had been given his salary, while the others, who continued to work, did not receive a penny; the directors, in the meantime had gone bankrupt.... He added that he had also painted an immense fresco for the Moulin Rouge: two Pierrots in the style of Willette, destroyed by the fire some years ago.[33]

Unfortunately, none of these works have survived. These activities demonstrate Maillol's involvement in the artistic subculture of his time and also provide evidence of some experiences on large-scale works of art other than *Far from the City* [*Loin de la ville*], a five-meter-long painting which he created during this epoch.

During these years of study in Paris, Maillol never lost contact with his native land. He customarily returned to Banyuls each summer for a period of time. In the summer of 1893, Maillol went to Banyuls for his annual visit, but remained there until 1895.

He had become interested in the art of tapestry while in Paris. He told Cladel, that he had spent entire afternoons at the Musée de Cluny studying medieval tapestries. Upon his arrival in Banyuls, he established a tapestry workshop from his own funds with five or six local girls as workers. He eventually fell in love with one of these young women, Clotilde, and married her in the spring of 1895.

The period from 1893 to 1895 was particularly fruitful for Maillol's artistic development. He designed many tapestry cartoons; he supervised the needlework of the girls in the atelier; he developed plant dyes and obtained unprocessed, handwoven wool thread from the peasants of the area for use in his tapestries. Lack of patronage finally forced him to close down the workshop in 1895 and return to Paris.

Since Maillol, himself, did not actually do any needlework on the tapestries, he sought some activity for his idle hands during the work sessions. He began carving directly in wood, with a knife, i.e., whittling. This primitive art is the "naive decoration, practiced since earliest times by the shepherds, at knife point."[34] In this almost accidental activity, we see the very beginnings of Maillol's career as a serious sculptor.

"Remembering his modeling exercises at the Ecole des Arts Décoratifs, . . . he took up the rustic pocket knife of the artist-artisan and began to carve pieces of wood; walnut, pear, or olive."[35] During this very early stage in his sculptural career, he carved both bas-reliefs, and pieces of sculpture in the round.

Woodcarving was not the only new "medium" in which Maillol experimented at this time: "He discovered around Banyuls . . . a clay bed 'as fine and malleable' as commercial clay."[36] Perhaps this virtually free source of clay was the reason for a burst of activity in the medium. We know that his interest in the art of ceramics only increased during the following years.

Maillol returned to Paris to live with his new wife in the spring of 1895. It seems likely that he became personally acquainted with the Nabis[37] around this time. The only solid bit of evidence we have concerning the date Maillol was brought into contact with the Nabis appears in a letter from Maillol to Rippl-Ronai,[38] dated September 14, 1894. This is the earliest preserved letter of their correspondence.[39] "I was very happy to learn that the young artists have come to see you. I do not know them, but I hope to make their acquaintance through you this year." One knows of no other group of "young artists" (Denis was nine years younger than Maillol) with whom Rippl-Ronai was in contact at this time, other than the Nabis. Further on in this letter Maillol states that he does not expect to return to Paris until January 15, 1895, at the earliest, but it is much more likely that he did not come to the capital until the spring of 1895, after his marriage. He would probably have met the Nabis shortly after his arrival in Paris, since they were meeting frequently in Rippl's studio at this time.[40]

The date of 1895 for this meeting between Maillol and the Nabis would coincide with comments made by Bonnard and Denis recalling their friendship with Maillol. Denis wrote: "He [Maillol] was certainly not in the first group of this name [Nabi] between '89 and '93, those from the Academie Julian, and he did not take part in our dinners in the Passage Brady."[41]

Bonnard confirms this later date, i.e. 1895, for his acquaintance with Maillol when he states:

> As one knew artists, twenty or thirty years ago, sharing the same aspirations, I met Maillol and other friends. He made tapestries with very delicate harmonies. He was already a man close to nature, dying the wools himself and carving wood in imitation of Gauguin.[42]

As far as one knows Maillol began sculpting in wood only around 1894-95. In any case, he had surely met the Nabis by 1896 when he participated, for the first time in the group's private exhibition in the gallery of the Barc de Boutteville.

Between 1895 and 1898, Maillol was active, artistically, in a wide variety of media. He created tapestries, ceramics, woodcuts, lithographs and wooden sculpture, both free standing and in relief. He also drew constantly, producing many drawings, mostly of clothed and nude female figures. He painted infrequently; *The Wave* (fig. 14) and *The Mediterranean* (fig. 15) date from this period. He always carried a small notebook, in which he would execute quick sketches from life. This was a habit he maintained throughout his life, eventually filling hundreds of notebooks. This practice was a continuation of his training at the Ecole des Beaux-Arts where instructors always advised students to carry such a notebook.[43]

After 1893, Maillol exhibited regularly at the Salon Nationale des Beaux-Arts. He showed both tapestries and sculpted wood and ceramic objects. It seems that his bursting power of creativity was constrained only by a lack of money to pay for supplies. Vollard recalls that Maillol turned to sculpture when he could no longer afford canvas and paints. The artist remained extremely poor. In the autumn of 1897 the young ménage moved from 282 Rue St. Jacques to much cheaper living quarters in the suburb of Villeneuve St. Georges. He now became the neighbor of Denis, Vuillard, and Roussel. His intimate friendships with these men date from this time.

Since Maillol had no personal financial resources, patronage was essential to him. Vuillard introduced him to two patrons, Prince Antoine Bibesco and Ambrose Vollard. Each was to prove crucial for Maillol's artistic development, the former in relation to Maillol's tapestry production, the latter with regard to his sculpture.

Prince Bibesco, his mother, and his brother were very enthusiastic about Maillol's tapestries. They commissioned three tapestries, *Music* (1896-97) (fig. 25); *Music for a Bored Princess* (1897) (fig. 26); and *The Bather* (1898-1900) (fig. 27).

With the generous patronage of the Bibescos, Maillol had enough money to purchase a loom, making it possible for him to create truely woven tapestries, as opposed to the embroidery or "petit-point" technique which he had previously been forced to use. He set up his loom in Banyuls and began to work. A third of the tapestry was done when he suffered an attack of blindness, resulting from the strain to his eyes from the meticulous labor. This was around 1900. He lost his eyesight completely for six months and was warned that to continue working would provoke a recurrence of the malady. All that remains of his final endeavor are two cartoons (fig. 28).[44] Maillol summarized this period of his career in the following way: "The epoch of the tapestries was the happiest of my life."[45]

As Maillol's career as a tapestry-maker was tragically ending, his career as a sculptor was really only beginning. Ambrose Vollard bought several of Maillol's terra-cotta statuettes and cast them in bronze editions which sold well. This finally provided Maillol with a steady source of income. Later on Maillol said of this period, "It was thanks to Vollard that I could live."[46]

Prior to the appearance of Vollard on the scene, Maillol had improvised methods for baking his clay statuettes. Monfreid had recorded in his journal on May 5, 1897: "Upon returning, I found Maillol who tried to bake some pottery in my oven which soon cracked."[47] Vollard built a kiln for Maillol at Villeneuve St. Georges. Undoubtedly the three fountains (now in the Vierny collection, figs. 32 and 33) were baked in the Villeneuve kiln. From this time on, Maillol virtually ceased his activity as a painter and devoted himself exclusively to sculpture, progressing from small statuettes to over-life-sized works.

In 1902, Maillol had his first one-man show at Vollard's gallery. He exhibited several tapestries and smaller embroidered works, as well as his ceramics and small bronzes. This show received some favorable reviews:

> Without energetic effort, a robust art. Without ostentious honesty, a sincere art...this pagan aesthetic is here renewed by the carelessness of regular lines of geometrically measured profiles. It is modern...and these are remarkable tapestries...this is an achievement without violence, with a very happy composition where a rare decorative skill is confirmed.[48]

Rodin also visited the show, and was so impressed with Maillol's bronzes that he purchased one for himself and told Octave Mirbeau about his enthusiasm for the "new" sculptor.[49]

From this time on, Maillol was well established as an independent artist. In 1904, he moved from Villeneuve to Marly-le-Roi. There he set up the studio which he maintained as a summer workshop for the rest of his life. His life now assumed a pattern which would continue without interruption until his death (with the exception of the periods of the two world wars). Winters were spent in Banyuls, summers at Marly-le-Roi.

The plaster version of *La Méditerranée,* the first of the large-scaled pieces of sculpture was exhibited at the Salon d'Automne in 1905. For the next forty years, until he died following an automobile accident in 1944, Maillol devoted himself to the large-scaled pieces of sculpture for which he is famous. It is a very limited oeuvre of about twenty major creations, focused on the unvarying theme of the female nude. He also was quite active as a book illustrator.

Toward the end of his life, in the late 1930s, Maillol returned to painting for his own enjoyment and relaxation. These works are very stiff, rather academic exercises, lacking the charm and beauty of the best of his paintings of the 1890s. However, they document his love of painting, which continued despite the thirty years he spent as a sculptor.

2

The Paintings

Early Works: 1888-91

Maillol's career as a painter is concentrated between the years 1888, when he was twenty-seven years old, and 1898. Through the paintings which have survived, one can trace his evolution from a recent graduate of the Ecole des Beaux-Arts, copying older nineteenth-century masters, and searching for a personal style, to a young artist wanting to throw off the lessons of the past and desperately seeking more modern sources of inspiration, to a mature artist secure in his own iconography and techniques. Through a process of experimentation with a variety of painterly modes, Maillol eventually developed an appropriate style and iconography with which he could express his vision of the female body. In sculpture this would become his personal statement, his contribution to the history of art.

The dates of this activity coincide with a very exciting period of discovery for the avant-garde painters of France. The first Impressionist exhibition in 1874 had heralded, to the Parisian public at least, a new form for recording the most fleeting aspects of nature. The decade of the 1880s was a period of "explicit experimentalism"[1] for a new generation of painters as well as for the Impressionists themselves, who were reevaluating the premises upon which their achievements of the 1860s and 1870s had been based. By the late 1880s, Van Gogh, Gauguin, and Cézanne, among others, had abandoned the Impressionist goal of capturing in as impersonally accurate a manner as possible passing appearances of the world around them for other goals, which, while all different, stressed the individual painter's reaction to this study of nature.

The fundamental premise that the artist should dedicate himself to the depiction of the real world was to be seriously questioned, if not consistently explored in paint, by Gauguin and Bernard at Pont Aven in 1888. By the early 1890s a group of young painters had gathered around Sérusier in the Atelier Julian. They called themselves the Nabis (the Hebrew word for prophets). Members of the group, which included Denis, Sérusier, Ranson, Vuillard, and

Roussel, codified the doctrine that painting must no longer represent merely the appearance of the external world.

Maurice Denis was the most important theoretician of his generation. At this point in the history of art, he and his circle were reacting against both academicism and Impressionism. Therefore it was important and necessary to assert forcefully the belief that Art, while utilizing elements from nature, was not meant to reproduce the images the artist receives through his eyes:

> They [the Nabis] had the great capacity to scorn the foolish prejudice upheld everywhere, and so pernicious to artists of yesterday, that it is sufficient for the painter to copy what he sees, stupidly, as he sees it, that a painting is an open window on nature, and that, finally, art lies in the exactitude of the rendering.[2]

Albert Aurier, among others, forcefully stated this disdain for the naturalistic artist in his crucial and widely read article, "Les Peintres symbolistes" published in 1892:

> The myopic copy of social anecdotes, the imbecilic imitation of the warts of nature, flat observation, the trompe l'oeil, the glory of being as faithfully, as banally, exact as a daguerreotype, will not satisfy any painter, any sculptor worthy of these names.[3]

To the Symbolists, the Impressionists were as misguided as their academic predecessors. The Impressionists, in attempting to capture the effects of atmosphere and light were seeking to copy the visual impressions of the external world.

Denis exempts from condemnation "two or three painters of genius," but condemns Impressionism which implies that "the absence of method must be the external sign of individual sincerity, of temperament."[4]

In place of Naturalism, "stupid imitation," in his phrase, Denis sought to return art to what he considered to be its true traditions prior to the High Renaissance. The art of the Egyptians, Greeks, and the Middle Ages, to cite a few examples, were not naturalistic images but the emotional, creative deformation of nature for expressive purposes. The importance of referring back to the history of pre-Renaissance western art as well as non-western sources was so compelling that originally Denis wanted to give the name *Neo-traditionalism* to the new movement.[5]

By 1909, when a certain historical perspective could be established, Denis published "From Gauguin and Van Gogh to Classicism." In this article, Denis saw the major impetus behind the works of the best artists of his generation, particularly Cézanne, Gauguin, and Van Gogh, to be directed toward a "new classical order." The main criterion for this modern manifestation of classicism was the existence in the work of a proper balance between naturalistic appearances and the artist's personal response to nature: "All beautiful works contain a certain equilibrium between subjectivity and objectivity,—between ideal nature revealed by our artistic sense, and the reality which our reason understands."[6] Stated in another way Denis says that the classical artist "allows the proper equilibrium between nature and style, between expression and harmony."[7]

Maillol's works, his paintings, tapestries and sculpture must be viewed against this background. The Symbolist movement which developed into neo-classicism was the crucial formative influence for his personal style. Recognizing this, Denis placed Maillol, in his article of 1905, with those artists who achieve the proper classical balance necessary for great art: "Maillol took part in the neo-classical movement whose recent origins are to be found with Cézanne and Gauguin."[8]

An analysis of Maillol's development as a painter can be made from the surviving works, despite the unfortunate fact that many paintings have been lost. We know that Maillol did not concern himself with the fate of his artistic creations, once they had passed out of his direct control. Cladel asked Maillol about the location of an important painting executed thirty years earlier. He responded, with characteristic indifference, "I know nothing about it. I gave it away."[9] The group of paintings under discussion have survived, therefore, despite Maillol's relaxed attitude toward them, and not because he chose to retain these specific works. Other paintings have come to light because their owners had more respect for them than Maillol himself.

Aside from some juvenalia (such as the painting of a port[10]) the earliest known painting is a *Self-Portrait* (fig. 1) from 1888 of which Maillol, himself said: "I did not execute my portrait too badly; I was then influenced by Courbet."[11] Maillol presents himself in a three-quarter view against a nonspecific dark background. He reveals his debt to Courbet through the predominant use of earth tones, the strong contrast between areas of light and shadow and the thick, forceful application of paint. There are none of the props often found in painter's self-portraits: no brushes gripped in hand, no canvases piled in the background, nothing to indicate what profession this young man pursues. One wonders if the lack of these accoutrements reflects the artist's insecurity about his own personality as a painter, even, perhaps, a questioning of his potential to become an artist?

Another portrait, of Dr. Bassères, a life-long friend and supporter from Banyuls, appears to be executed in the same spirit. Here the sitter is placed very close to the picture surface and is similarly presented in a three-quarter view. As in Maillol's *Self-Portrait,* Bassères is positioned against a very dark background and there is a sharp division of the canvas into relatively large areas of light and darkness.

Maillol told Cladel that during his years of study at the Ecole des Beaux-Arts, he often copied works of the artists he admired.[12] There is certainly nothing surprising in this activity. From the moment a young painter entered an atelier, even before he reached the Ecole des Beaux-Arts, he was set to copy engravings. Later, he progressed to the copying of plaster casts and paintings in the Louvre. The entire academic curriculum was based upon the principle of copying. Copying works by revered masters was considered to be an absolutely essential part of a complete artistic education.[13] Therefore, as part of his curriculum, Maillol was made to copy works by Chardin, Fragonard, and Rembrandt in the Louvre.[14] The only two exact copies by Maillol which have survived, however, are after famous compositions by Puvis de Chavannes, *Poor Fisherman* and *Pastoral Scene (The Childhood of St. Geneviève)*. Possibly, the immediate impetus for Maillol's study of Puvis de Chavannes was the major retrospective of his paintings at the Durand-Ruel Gallery during November and December 1887. Practically all of Puvis's major easel paintings and small-scaled versions of his mural cycles were included in this exhibition. On this occasion, the government purchased *The Poor Fisherman,* which was then hung in the Luxembourg Museum. (The St. Geneviève murals had been in place in the Panthéon since 1878.)

Maillol's copies were probably painted during the last year of his tenure at the Ecole des Beaux-Arts in 1888 or early in 1889, in the spirit of an academic exercise. After this date, as Maillol matured, his borrowings from other artists took the form of adaptations of one or another aspects of the admired work rather than literal copies.

The existence of these two copies are tangible manifestations of Maillol's regard for Puvis. Many years later, Maillol reaffirmed the importance of the older master's painting for him in his formative years:

> Puvis! It was for him that we had the greatest emotions of art in our youth: these compositions in a pretty style with beautiful drawings filled us with the impression of poetry in their science of spacious décor and their harmony. The works of Puvis were a good recommendation for our inexperience.[15]

Maillol was certainly not the only artist to study Puvis. Many artists of his generation incorporated Puvis's formal devices, such as the frieze composition, shallow space and matte tonalities, into their works. Puvis was the most important source for these artists seeking to explore the decorative possibilities of painting.[16] The fact that Maillol, in searching for models, turned to works by Puvis is a significant clue for understanding the artistic goals toward which he was striving.

> His [Puvis de Chavannes's] influence is to be observed above all among those Symbolists who wished to devote themselves to modern ideas, without thereby losing all contact with the orthodox tradition of the academies.

The Nabis—who were moderate by temperament and, anxious to savour all the achievements of art, aimed at reconciling the most audacious ideas with respect for tradition—made a positive cult of Puvis."[17]

Therefore, Maillol's goals for painting paralleled those of the Nabis. Like them, Maillol also was a "moderate by temperament." Maillol had not yet met any of the Nabi group. The later meetings and strong friendships which developed between Maillol and Denis, Roussel and Vuillard are by no means accidental or fortuitous, but predetermined by a common interest in a renovation of Art toward the same goals in the same historical epoch.

Puvis's art embodied certain concepts which would be crucial to the formation of Maillol's painting style. The older master utilized elements of reality, depicted in a personal stylistic idiom, to create a poetic image infused with symbolic meanings. The method by which Puvis realized these forms was primarily the *Synthèse:* the use of nonspecific, simplified forms (rather than an anecdotal, precise description of any specific specimen of reality) arranged in a "decorative" fashion. Thus he achieved the balance between nature and the imagination which Denis described as the basic requirement for classical Art.

The first paintings Maillol created after he had left the Ecole des Beaux-Arts, during the years 1889 to 1891, are works of a technically proficient artist, as were most Ecole graduates, but one absolutely lacking a personal style. Therefore his earliest paintings clearly reveal the strong impression made on the young man by the paintings of Puvis de Chavannes, and the other most significant figure for Maillol, Gauguin.

One group of paintings which must date from 1889 to 1891 reveals the influence of Gauguin's Breton landscape style: *The Prodigal Son, Girl Tending Cows* (fig. 2) and *Girl with a Goat.* These paintings depict a small-scaled figure on either the far right or far left, positioned in a landscape.

According to Rewald, the works of Puvis were not sufficiently forceful to provide the impetus necessary to set Maillol on an individual path. This is undoubtedly true. While Maillol might have greatly admired Puvis's works, he could not use them as a guide toward a personal mode of expression. Gauguin's paintings could fill this need.

"Gauguin's painting was a revelation to me," said Maillol. "L'Ecole des Beaux-Arts, instead of leading me to the light, had led me away from it. When I looked at Gauguin's pictures of Pont-Aven, I felt inspired by the same spirit which had prompted his work: and I told myself at once that what I was doing would be satisfactory if Gauguin were to approve of it."[18]

At another time, speaking of this period, he reiterated the significance of Gauguin for the evolution of his artistic style: "It has been said that, at the beginning of my career, I was influenced by Gauguin's sculpture in wood: that is a legend. He was useful to me, but only in painting."[19] Although Maillol might have seen isolated works by Gauguin during the winter of 1889 (Gauguin was living in Paris from December 1888, following his stay in Arles, to April 1889), the Café Volpini show, which opened in late May 1889, provided his first opportunity for an intensive study of a group of Gauguin's paintings.

On this occasion, Gauguin exhibited seventeen paintings: seven were landscapes, five from Brittany and two from his brief stay with Van Gogh in Arles. Gauguin's landscapes from this period often had one or two small-scale human figures and an occasional animal. They were executed in a system of fairly short parallel brushstrokes of highly saturated colors (a method of paint application adapted from Cézanne). Examples of this specific type of landscape are *Winter* (W. 258), *The Pig Herder* (W. 354), *The Farm Gate* (W. 353), or *The Blonde Harvest* (W. 351).[20] In all these works, the figures are clearly subordinated to a broad, colorful landscape. Only *Winter* was exhibited at the Café Volpini show, but Maillol had access to other canvases of this type, such as *The Blonde Harvest* and *The Farm Gate,* since they belonged to his friend de Monfreid.

Significantly, Gauguin's *Vision after the Sermon* was not exhibited on this occasion. This painting, "detaches itself very strongly from the main drift of Gauguin's development during 1888 . . . it was not until the opening year of his first stay in Tahiti that he would turn back to the structure of the *Vision* and exploit its potential afresh."[21] During 1888 and 1889 Gauguin was still working primarily in a fractured technique of parallel, Cézanne-like, brushstrokes as opposed to the broad uninterrupted planes of colors encircled by the black lines of true "Cloisonisme."[22] But Maillol must have seen this painting in Gauguin's studio, since one of the cows in *Girl Tending Cows* is borrowed directly from Gauguin's *Vision.*

In all three paintings by Maillol, foreground, middle ground, and background areas contain objects properly reduced in scale. Spatial recession is indicated through the use of flat planes set at different points in space, but remaining parallel to the picture plane. Therefore, the viewer perceives depth through a horizontal eye movement back and forth for each plane.

In *Girl Tending Cows* (fig. 2) those flat parallel planes take on more curving shapes:

> At first glance, the picture space seems to be clearly organized by layers. The girl and dog occupy the first plane, then other natural forms take the eye back through the landscape in successive planes. The viewer may become aware of a counterpoint to this layering in slow-curving diagonals which go from lower left to upper right in the painting, dividing it into amorphous "organic" shapes.[23]

It seems likely that Maillol was adapting this treatment of space from Gauguin's Breton landscapes, which often use a similar type of flattened space with a very high horizon line.

Like Gauguin's images, the paint is applied in a series of short, feathery and parallel brushstrokes, in these early paintings by Maillol. However, Maillol had not forgotten his study of Puvis de Chavannes. Traces of that artist appear in a number of ways, particularly in *Girl Tending Cows:* "...the drawing of the figure, the lilac in the skirt, the flat planes, and the use of flowers to the right of the girl all are adaptations by Maillol of Puvis' usages."[24] Although the presence of these factors confirm Maillol's assimilation of Puvis's techniques, more interestingly, Wattenmaker notes that "making the bottom of the skirt a kind of platform is... 'Puvisesque'" as well.[25] The bottom of the skirt does function in a way similar to the base of a piece of sculpture, and perhaps one can posit an early association in Maillol's mind of the possibility of sculpting a meditative figure which would become, eventually, *The Mediterranean.*[26]

Surely the emotional quality of quiet sadness exuding from all three of these paintings can be traced to Puvis. One need only think of *The Poor Fisherman* to see how that master managed to convey similar emotions without exaggerated gestures, contorted facial expressions or any form of theatricality. In the specific case of *The Prodigal Son* it is likely that Maillol's idea for the subject came from a painting by Puvis of the same title which was shown at the Durand-Ruel show, in 1887.[27] However, in Puvis's image the figure dominates the picture space, with the landscape clearly relegated to a secondary position. The opposite is true in the Maillol, which connects it more closely with the series of landscapes by Gauguin.

The figures in *The Prodigal Son* and *Girl Tending Cows* (fig. 2) are both seated with head bent down, supported by a hand braced on one knee. It is quite possible that Maillol was initially influenced in the choice of position for his figures by Emile Bernard's drawing, *Rêverie,* published in the catalogue from the Café Volpini show (1889). In Bernard's image a woman in Breton costume is seated in a landscape, with her head bent in meditation as the title suggests. This figure is rendered in a highly simplified, or rather synthesized, style; only a few strong lines define her form. Similarly, Maillol's women are also rendered in a vigorously simplified style. In addition, they are rather mysterious figures unexplained by the context in which they are placed. The viewer cannot possibly know who they are, where they are or what they are thinking. Both Maillol's and Bernard's figures seem removed from the world they inhabit and the viewer's world as well. They are turned completely inward, sunk in meditation.

This sense of quiet, mysterious ambiguity is a consciously sought quality and will be present in virtually all Maillol's future works. We have already noted the close relationship between these paintings and Gauguin's and Bernard's *Pont-Aven* style in terms of the selected subjects, the depiction of the figures, and the flattened landscape space. These works are also related to the contemporary movement of Symbolism in literature.

Maurice Maeterlinck, a Symbolist playwright, writing in *Le Figaro* (1894), attempted to define the nature of a Symbolist work of art, on the occasion of seeing an Ibsen play at the Théâtre de l'Oeuvre, *Solness le Constructeur*. He says that a "good" painter would not paint an isolated event in history but rather:

> He would represent a house lost in the countryside, an open door at the end of a corridor, a face or hands at rest; and these simple images could add something to our consciousness of life; that which is goodness, which is impossible to lose.... [28]

Maillol's images, like those Maeterlinck mentions, are designed to stimulate a similar contemplative mood on the part of the viewer. Like so many other works of the period, they are meant to be ambiguous so that the viewer must exercise his own imagination to try to understand the meaning behind the bare image presented.

All Maillol's figures seem closed into themselves; only rarely do their eyes confront the viewer. They are not specific objective correlatives, but rather examples of Mallarmé's famous dictum:

> To name an object, is to suppress three-quarters of the enjoyment of the poem which is created by the gradual pleasure of apprehending it. To suggest it, that is the dream. It is the perfect use of this mystery which constitutes the symbol; to evoke bit by bit an object to show a state of soul."[29]

Beauty in art, according to Symbolist doctrine, resides in the suggestion and implication of emotions, not in their precise delineation. Maillol's images are sufficiently imprecise, but intriguing enough to fit in perfectly with Mallarmé's requisites for art.

The subjects of *Girl with a Goat* and *Girl Tending Cows* are early manifestations of the theme which will dominate Maillol's painting virtually to the exclusion of all other subjects: the female figure placed in a landscape setting. During the next few years, Maillol explored the ways in which the form of a woman can be integrated with, or juxtaposed to, growing vegetal life. In fact, Maillol never painted a woman without including at least a tree, some foliage, or a flowered background. Maillol's painted women are creatures who live, as Maillol himself, in close contact with growing vegetation; trees and flowers. They are not instinctive, non-thinking creatures, but natural beings, linked by their essential natures with the vegetal world about them.

A basis for further speculation on the symbolic meaning of these paintings is provided by the haystacks in *Girl with a Goat* and *Girl Tending Cows* (fig. 2). Both Gauguin and Bernard painted several harvest scenes or landscapes with haystacks during their Brittany sojourns, and the inclusion of haystacks might simply be another case of their influence on Maillol. However, a level of symbolic correspondence can be projected between these young women who have reached physical maturity, but have not yet been consumed by the passions of love and the burdens of womanhood, and the ripe hay harvested and soon to be consumed to perpetuate the life cycle of the cattle. The mammalian form of the haystack with its connotations of maternal fertility and nourishment supports a symbolic interpretation of the paintings.

The traditional associations between Death, personified as a reaper and the harvest are also quite easily revived by these contemplative figures seated in the harvested fields, and one is encouraged by the mood of these paintings to ponder them.

We are fortunate to have a definite date for the *Portrait of Jeanne Sarrail* (fig. 3). It was exhibited in the official Salon de la Société des Artistes Français, in 1890. The sitter appears to be about twelve years old. As far as we know, it is the largest, most ambitious work Maillol created, to date (148.5 x 101.5 cm).

The portrait is executed in a tight system of parallel brushstrokes, visible throughout the canvas, except in the rendition of the dress. The figure stands in the horizontal and vertical center of the picture space, on a richly patterned Oriental carpet, in front of pink grounded, floral patterned wallpaper. Her eyes confront the viewer directly and unselfconsciously.

Significantly, the only other object in the painting is a large potted plant, placed upon a floor cushion. I believe that, even at this early date, Maillol felt it was impossible to paint an image of a young female without the presence of a part of living, vegetal nature. Moreover, the plant serves a decorative function: the broad, spiky outline of the leaves provides a visual link to both the more geometricized beige, orange, and blue leaf-shapes of the carpet and the flowers in the wallpaper.

It seems unlikely that Maillol would have chose an interior *venue* himself since this is his only painting which is set in an interior space, and perhaps this reflects the choice of the patron. His preference for relating the figure to a natural setting thwarted, Maillol felt the need to establish the presence of nature, however cultivated it might be. The cushion upon which the pot rests was undoubtedly needed to raise the level of the plant so that the highest leaves reach to Jeanne's shoulder. (We are not given any other objective standard against which to measure her height.) In this way, the plant's height can compete with the natural height of the sitter. A silent dialogue commences between the flourishing beauty of the plant and the strong, upright posture of Jeanne Sarrail.

The flowers in the pattern of the wallpaper provide another "natural" element in this closed interior. Bunches of white flowers are distributed across the pink background in such a way as to frame Jeanne, creating an aureole about her. Flowered wallpaper was often used by the Impressionists to give continuity to the wall behind the sitter which would "implicitly go on beyond the framing edges."[30] Degas used flowered wallpaper as a background for his *Portrait of Hortense Valpinçon* (1871-72)—a girl about as old as Jeanne—and Gauguin adapted this motif for his *Self-Portrait—Les Misérables,* of 1888. In a letter to Van Gogh, Gauguin explained the wallpaper flowers of the background as "a delicate maidenly background with its childlike flowers."[31] The connotation of this particular background is clear: it stands for virginity, for sheltered, protected domesticity. It is the objective correlative for our sitter who is on the brink of sexual knowledge, but still young enough to be content with her child's world. That both Gauguin and Maillol could adapt it for their own paintings shows that this motif had become part of a symbolic language by 1890.

Up until this time, Maillol's works were relatively small easel paintings. Probably during the summer of 1891, he painted a very large canvas entitled *Far from the City (Loin de la ville).* Maillol described the circumstances surrounding the creation of this work to Cladel:

> During a stay in Fécamp, where I was giving drawing lessons to a group of American women, I commenced a five meter wide canvas of them, entitled *Far from the City.* These young women were beautiful, bursting with life and health; they wore large hats, following the style of that year; I made a considerable effort.[32]

Although the mural is lost, another painting, *Woman with an Umbrella* (fig. 4), if not actually a part of the mural must have been painted during the same summer in a very similar spirit.

Woman with an Umbrella depicts a young woman dressed in contemporary costume, wearing a broad-brimmed hat, corresponding to Maillol's description. The woman is placed before the sea. (Fécamp is a seaside resort.) The canvas is almost two meters tall, so it is on the same scale as *Far from the City.*

The young woman stands in a strict profile position before a background which is divided into layers to indicate charcoal gray earth, white sand, blue sea, and pearl gray sky. Her left hand is raised to steady her broad-brimmed hat. Her lowered right hand holds a parasol down at her side.

In the background, the paint is applied very freely; one can see the brushwork throughout. The figure itself is executed in a more controlled, smaller pattern of brushstrokes. The contour of the model's form is clearly defined against the background of whites and blues. This image is not a quick sketch, designed to capture a specific movement, but a carefully worked out, studied composition: a formal image frozen in a determined attitude.

The background in *Woman with an Umbrella* does not attempt to copy the appearance of reality, but presents a view of the sea that is an abstract decorative pattern of parallel bands of color. This gives the viewer the impression of seeing a figure set before a flat backdrop; the sea does not recede back into space. However, Maillol has integrated the figure and ground compositionally. The horizontal division between sea and sky coincides exactly with the horizontal line dividing the woman's hair and forehead. At the point where sea is divided from sand, the tips of the woman's left hand touch the parasol. The only irregularity in the straight lines separating the colors occurs in the division between gray earth and white sand. Maillol has extended the gray color to fill the negative space between parasol and dress. (Cézanne does a similar filling in of a background color in his *Nude Bather* [Museum of Modern Art, New York].)

In this work, Maillol has directly attacked one of the most consuming problems of the second half of the nineteenth century—the integration of a figure and a landscape, and has arrived at a pleasing, original solution. Furthermore, his image of reality has been subjected to a process of consistent simplification which will be critical for his subsequent development. This is the essential component of Denis's definition of classical art: There is "no classical artist who is not economical with his means, who does not subordinate all the graces of detail to the beauty of the whole... "[33]

Maillol's figure is close in spirit to the promenading woman on the far right in Seurat's *La Grande Jatte*. The model shares with Seurat's figure a strict profile position which prevents the viewer's attempts at psychological penetration. Both figures are dressed in modern costume and there is a similar interest in the articulation of a clearly defined, simplified, outline: a smoothly flowing, easily discernible contour. Even the motif of a parasol is present in both works.

It is not necessary to posit a direct influence from Seurat to Maillol (although it is certainly possible that a direct influence might exist). It could well be another case of two artists reacting to the same initial model, Puvis de Chavannes. We know that Seurat was influenced by Puvis's monumental mural style. In fact Félix Fénéon refers to *La Grande Jatte* as a "modernized Puvis."[34] The gesture of Maillol's woman holding her brim has a similar quality to Puvis's central figure in *Women by the Sea* (Louvre, Paris), who holds and separates her long hair. Both gestures turn inwards, making the figures completely self-contained. They are not expressive either, providing no clues to the emotional state or the psychology of the depicted women. Both figures convey the feeling of frozen immobility (also shared by the figure in *La Grande Jatte*). There is a sense of inevitability about them; these gestures are not insignificant, they have been carefully selected, and, yet, their meaning remains ambiguous.

In addition to these contemporary sources, a number of elements in *Woman with an Umbrella* reveal a knowledge of Quattrocento painting. The elegant linear contour of the figure, the deliberate integration of figure and background and the decorative swirl of the ribbons are common motifs in Early Renaissance painting.[35] Maillol could have found all these elements in

Ghirlandaio's frescoes in the choir of Santa Maria Novella. One figure in the *Birth of the Baptist* raises her hand to steady a basket of fruit on her head, using the same gesture as Maillol's woman. As we shall see, Early Renaissance painting will become an increasingly important source for Maillol's subsequent paintings.

The Profile Portraits: 1891-94

Between 1891 and 1894, Maillol created a series of paintings which present (with several exceptions) a single bust-length female figure, positioned in profile, hair coiffed in the contemporary style of a chignon, set against a very simple backdrop. In the first group of works, the background is chrome yellow. In the second group, it is foliated. But in all these paintings the background is flat, preventing any movement back into space.

One profile image, now in the Musée de Reims, is conveniently dated 1891 (fig. 5). A terminal date for these paintings is late 1894, or the first few months of 1895, when Maillol painted the *Portrait of Mme. Maillol* (fig. 10), which in several respects is quite different from this group: type of background, method of modeling, the three-quarter view, and the relationship between figure and ground. Since we can date that work rather securely, it thus provides us with a terminus ante quem for these paintings.

There is additional data which confirms the dates 1891 to 1894 for the group. Perhaps the most carefully worked canvas of this period was the *Portrait of Aunt Lucie,* one of the two maiden aunts who raised Maillol. Although the present location of this work is unknown, we have two descriptions of it. During Maillol's later years, it was prominently hung in the dining room of the pink house in Banyuls:

> She is seen in profile, seated, thin and tall; her expression has the authority and tenderness of an old spinster."[36]

> A thin silhouette, clothed in black, seated in profile before a background of sky and trees, the head with austere features pressed by a narrow cap of transparent organdy, hand on her knees, she is in an imposingly dignified attitude, a type of mistress of the house, half-bourgeois, half-peasant, such as exists in the region of the Pyrenees.[37]

Dr. Bassères places this work in time between 1892 *(The Portrait of Abbè Rous)*[38] and late 1894-95 *(The Portrait of Mme. Maillol).* From these descriptions, it is clear that this is still another example of the profile formula.

The artist himself provided some information about this painting. Apparently he showed it to Gauguin and quoted Gauguin's comment; "It is good, but dry." Since we know that Gauguin was in Europe between his two trips to Tahiti, from September 1893 to July 1895, the portrait must have been painted between 1893 and 1894. But apart from these dates there is no concrete information upon which to base a precise chronology. The paintings have been grouped according to internal stylistic considerations, into a logical pattern.

The first four works to be considered are: *Profile of a Woman* (fig. 6), *Girl in Blue* (Gug. 4)[39], *Spring* (fig. 7), and *Crowned Child* (fig. 8). These paintings all depict very young, adolescent girls, in profile, set against a bright yellow background.

The half length profile portrait, as a formula, dates back at least to the early Italian Renaissance. Piero della Francesca's *Portraits of the Count and Countess of Urbino* are early examples of a formula which will become most common for portraits in the third quarter of the fifteenth century. The Renaissance portrait, as a type, is surely the underlying source for Maillol's paintings.

Borrowing from earlier art in this way was perfectly acceptable. As noted above, Denis was so concerned with the relation of modern art to earlier artistic formulas that he wanted the movement to be called *Neo-traditionalism*. Of the variety of types of art which constitute "the great art, which one calls decorative,"[40] the early Renaissance was the latest manifestation.

Of course Maillol might have seen contemporary equivalents of Quattrocento-type images. This period had been explored quite thoroughly by the Pre-Raphaelites. A modern evocation of the Renaissance profile portrait formula which is quite similar to Maillol's paintings was published in *Studio*, the magazine of the British Arts and Crafts movement that was circulated in France. In the November 1893 issue a line drawing entitled *La Ghirlandita* illustrates a plaster relief by R. Anning Bell. The figure is described by a very simple contour line and a few leaves are strung along one side. It is quite possible that Maillol could have seen this illustration although it appeared rather late to be a formative influence on his own series. He might easily have known similar British examples, since British works were regularly exhibited in the annual Parisian Salons, during this period.

Profile of a Woman (fig. 6) shares with the Reims portrait the oblique placement of the figure, shifted to one side of the picture space, and the ubiquitous tree balancing the figure on the other side. The pink dress of this sitter links it to earlier uses of pink in *Woman with an Umbrella* (fig. 4) and *Jeanne Sarrail* (fig. 3). While the Reims portrait (fig. 5) is a relatively straightforward image of a young woman in a simple everyday dress, the figure in the Perpignan *Profile* (fig. 6) wears a black hat crowned with artificial red roses. She is completely self-contained, her gaze is directed downwards, isolating her from the viewer to an even greater extent than is usual in Maillol's paintings. The model's body is undeveloped, pre-adolescent, poised between girlhood and womanhood. By contrast, the red and black hat ought to belong to a sophisticated woman. Maillol was surely exploiting this discordance to create his image. The contrast between *naïvete* and sophistication will be explored further in subsequent paintings.

Girl in Blue (Gug. 4) presents a definitely adolescent girl, in a three-quarter view, wearing a simple blue dress and set against a yellow background. Maillol's execution of the face is somewhat different here than in the other works discussed. The skin tone is composed of small separate touches of lime green, gold and beige. The colors are applied to a pale beige undertone in very tiny, even and parallel brushstrokes. The color mixture of the face suggests reflected sunlight filtered through green leaves. The painting remains a unique example, in Maillol's oeuvre, of this rather labored method. In contrast to the complexity of the face, the hair, dress and background are painted in flat, solid colors, while the bottom right portion of the painting has been left unfinished.

A likely explanation for the differences in the degree of finish as well as the unusual features of the face is that it was a study for a more complex work. That would account for the unfinished corner and the unusual, experimental treatment of the face. In fact, a painting now in Switzerland, *Spring* (fig. 7) shows the same standing brown-haired girl in the same three-quarter profile position as *Girl in Blue*. In *Spring,* she is paired with another girl in the familiar profile position, wearing a large hat quite similar to those in *Profile of a Woman* (fig. 6) and *Woman with an Umbrella* (fig. 4).

The two girls appear to be the same size and wear similarly styled dresses. In fact, it is possible that Maillol is actually using the same model twice. But there is a clear contrast between the open-eyed direct gaze of the girl on the left and the closed and isolated profile figure on the right. The simple wreath of the girl on the left is a "natural," unaffected ornament, in contrast to the elaborate artificial "city" hat of the figure in profile. I propose that the painting reveals Maillol's feelings towards the Parisians, in contrast to the women from his native land, Roussillon. The Parisians, especially the women, must have appeared to the shy young man to be inscrutable, unfriendly, and unapproachable. The provincial women of his experience were direct, without artifices, and open to sexual relationships (Maillol's wife was, of course, a native of Banyuls). Knowing Maillol's strong identification with his provincial homeland, his constantly renewing love of nature and his sensuality, one can easily imagine his loneliness, the sense of being "dépaysé" when he lived in Paris. Therefore, this work can be seen as an allegorical confrontation between Parisian and provincial society, or at least the women within each of those cultures.

Of course, a simpler interpretation could be applied to the image. If the clue given in the title *Spring* is pursued, one may view the work as an allegory of the seasons. Spring, warm and open, crowned with flowers, is personified by the country girl on the left while winter, aloof and icy moves off the stage.

The juxtaposition of two figures, similar in physical appearance, perhaps, but quite different in the emotional and sexual qualities they project was used by Gauguin in his woodcut *At the Black Rocks.* Maillol would certainly have known this image since it was printed on the cover of the catalogue of the Café Volpini exhibition (1889).

Christopher Gray has established convincingly that the meaning of Gauguin's *At the Black Rocks* lies in its sexual implications. The crouching figure is seen as a "symbol of fear and reluctance" while the figure on which Maillol's painting is based "abandons itself to the caresses of the mysterious sea." This interpretation is given credence by the presence of the black basalt rocks which in Brittany were the location for cult rituals performed to insure marriage and fertility.[41] While *At the Black Rocks,* cannot be considered a direct source for *Spring,* the basic idea for the format, which contrasts a yielding woman with an intractable one, can be traced to Gauguin's conception.

The distinct positions of the two figures in *Spring* serve to reinforce this interpretation. The country girl, on the left, seems to greet the viewer, or artist, directly; one can easily imagine her moving towards us. The girl on the right seems to be moving out of the picture space, away from the control of the artist, and out of our reach. She is, and will remain, unknowable, impossible to touch. Could she symbolize all those things which one believes to exist but which cannot be touched? Platonic Ideas, ideal love, religious faith; in short, all things of the spirit. The figure on the right, so tangible, could then be the symbol for those things we can know directly through our senses.

It should be noted that one can clearly see the presence of two distinct methods of paint application: the parallel, rhythmic strokes of the hat and hair of the girl on the left, and the broad areas of pure color of the dresses and yellow background which do not reveal individual strokes. We shall see that *Spring* is a transitional work between this group of paintings with yellow backgrounds and the subsequent group of profile images with foliated backgrounds.

The final painting of this yellow-background series, *Crowned Child* (fig. 8), is painted almost exclusively in simple, broad areas of pure color. In this painting a young girl in profile is placed against a very bright lemon yellow, daisy-studded background. On the far left, two tiny hands and a segment of pink skirt stand for a smaller child who is tying a garland of leaves and flowers around her head. There is an unreal, otherworldly mood to the painting. The model's eyes are closed and she seems to be sunk in concentration. The tying of this "crown" takes on the solemnity of a religious ceremony, a pagan rite of passage from childhood to womanhood. This interpretation is supported, I believe, by the outline of the girl's torso, which is shaped in a rounded curve, an arc, which, as in *Profile of a Woman* (fig. 6), is without the indication of breasts, but suggests a ripeness, a promise of physical blossoming.

A very important factor which unites all Maillol's paintings is the subject of women. Already, at this early phase of his development he has chosen the theme that will monopolize his creative energies for the rest of his life. Maillol's women all appear to be sensitive, delicate creatures. They are usually slender (this will change when he begins to make sculpture), adolescent or very young women. This choice of subject relates Maillol very closely to the contemporary literary movement of Symbolism and the images of the Nabis:

> ...the feminine subject was preferred [by the Nabis] to the masculine, as in Symbolist poetry, and it was the child-women, pale, slight, withdrawn which came closest to the spiritual ideal.[42]

Although many examples could be drawn from the poetry of the times to support this statement, I will quote the first stanza of a sonnet which Charles Morice (the author of the Symbolist manifesto of 1886) read at the Symbolist banquet of 1891. This was a semi-public affair, over which Mallarmé presided, given to honor Jean Moréas's publication of *Le Pèlerin Passioné*. The sonnet was quoted in full in the *Echo de Paris* of February 4, 1891:

> The beautiful girl without a care who lets us see,
> While dancing, the secret white of her pure throat...
> The pretty Artifice of a light despair...
> It is in your soul, beautiful singer, that she dances
> According to still unknown rites—and it is
> Her as Muse who selects your verses...
> The beautiful girl was your fantasy.[43]

"La Belle Fille," i.e. the beautiful girl, is the metaphor Morice has chosen to represent his source of inspiration: She is the personification of artistic creativity and the embodiment of the spirit behind Morice's works.[44]

This female type also recurs consistently in the paintings of the Nabis. One need only thumb through a group of illustrations of Nabi works from 1890 to 1895, to see the many slender, fragile young women, with pale necks, often dressed in white. This creature appears in Denis's works such as *Procession under the Trees, Sleeping Girl,* and *The Muses,* to cite only a few examples. Ranson's more sophisticated young women are equally evident in *Women in White* and *Women with Yellow Chrysanthemums.* Roussel's *Virgin on the Path* or Sérusier's *Incantation* are also peopled with these creatures.

In general, these women, depicted either singly or in groups are adolescent or just in the first blossoming of womanhood. They are innocent and virginal, sinless Eves before the fall. In Nabi paintings, "the figure is of interest not anatomically but rather as a vessel of the spirit. . . . Nudes are relatively rare."[45] There is very little depicted action. Figures often seem to be lost in private meditation and they are designed to stimulate the viewer to his own revery.[46]

It is precisely this type of "spiritual" young woman who sits, lost in contemplation, engaged in no action, which Maillol paints over and over. It is impossible to cite an exception. He is not creating naturalistic images of women, either in his paintings or, as we will see, in his tapestries. His women are artificially constructed and must be interpreted as spiritual beings: they are recognizable images of women as well as links to a nonmaterial world of contemplative meditation.

The avoidance of movement was an essential element of the symbolist aesthetic, later to be incorporated into Denis's "new classical order." Maillol's works in tapestry and sculpture, as well as in painting, share this absence of motion with virtually all Symbolist paintings of the decade. Further on in the article by Maeterlinck, quoted above, one reads: "... it has occurred to me to believe that this old, immobile man lives, in reality, a more profound, more human, and more universal life than the lover who strangles his mistress ... "[47] It is precisely these "immobile" images which Maillol, as well as Denis, Sérusier, Gauguin and Bernard, among many others of the avant garde, present for the viewer's contemplation.

The luminous yellow backgrounds of this group of paintings provides an interesting solution to the problem of a suitable backdrop: without actually describing an exterior, they imply or give the impression of bright sunlight. While Maillol wanted to situate these images in an outdoor setting, he also would have been concerned with not violating the flatness of the picture plane. (We have seen the way Maillol adapted some of Gauguin's techniques for depicting landscape space to achieve the same goal.) A flat backdrop of solid color would have the added advantage of not distracting the viewer's attention. Given these desires on the part of the artist, the use of a bright yellow backdrop provided a "kind of atmosphericity and luminous clarity that one associates with Monet's landscapes."[48] This comment was intended to describe Van Gogh's solid yellow backgrounds, but it also applies to Maillol's images. Although Van Gogh used his yellow backgrounds for still lifes or portraits, which were painted indoors, Maillol gave his backgrounds a much clearer context by the inclusion of a tree, and/or scattered leaf shapes positioned to one side.

A further distinction between the backgrounds of Maillol and those of Van Gogh is that Maillol intersperses small touches of white paint, which lightens the effect of the yellow, whereas Van Gogh always applies his paint very thickly, so that the brushstrokes are clearly visible. Despite these distinctions, Maillol was surely influenced in this respect by the paintings of Van Gogh. Several retrospective exhibitions of Van Gogh's paintings were held in Paris following the artist's death in 1891, and Maillol would have had sufficient opportunities to study them.[49]

The assertion of the flatness of the picture plane was one of the strongest priorities for all Symbolist artists of the time. Denis opened his first written codification of the theoretical foundations of the new art with the famous statement: "It is well to remember that a picture—before being a battle horse, a nude woman, or some anecdote—is essentially a plane surface covered with colors assembled in a certain order."[50] The movement away from a description of deep space is a widespread post-impressionist phenomenon which can be seen in canvases of the Impressionists as well as in those of Van Gogh and Gauguin. When comparing Renoir's *Large Bathers* (Tyson Collection) of 1884-87 with Gauguin's *Yellow Christ*, Roskill describes the landscape background in both paintings as "a continuous fabric hung parallel to the picture plane . . . while in the foreground heavy figures in stylized arrested poses join together in a common action."[51] This description is equally applicable to Maillol's images.

Maillol usually includes thin tree trunks with a scattering of green leaves, set to one side of his compositions. The leaves are usually widely dispersed, flattened out, and very nonspecific "organic" shapes. This motif can be traced directly to Gauguin's paintings. Gauguin often used leaves in a similar decorative manner, for example, in *Still Life with a Japanese Print* (W. 375, 1889). In this work, flattened leafy shapes are ranged along the lower edge of the painting.

In a series of works, Gauguin used the motif of a tree standing to the far right of the picture space with one branch jutting to the left and curving around the central figure.[52] Maillol's thin trees occupy the same position in his compositions and most often have the same single jutting branch.

The slender tree trunk with its few leaves becomes a symbol which immediately places the image outdoors, without a great deal of detailed description. The trees he uses are always very young, supple, and slender, providing a form in nature analogous to the youth and flexibility of the young women depicted.

In the next group of paintings, the feathery brushstrokes and the facture of the yellow background paintings is replaced by a technique employing large areas of unmodulated color. Each surface maintains its own local, flat and evenly applied color. Colors in general are more highly saturated. Three paintings form a further subdivision within this group: *Woman in Mauve, Girl with a Black Hat,* and *Two Girls* (fig. 9). These works have a unity of technique and intent and were most probably painted in close succession. Both *Woman in Mauve* and *Girl with a Black Hat* present the now familiar profile format. Both sitters are more mature women, rather than the budding girl-children of the preceding group. Technically, there is a marked tendency toward simplification and crystallization of the forms. Maillol is now using a more synthetic approach, a change which points to the influence of Maurice Denis.

Before 1891, Denis was using a pointillist technique. By 1892, however, he had switched to an increasingly simplified form, where each element is subjected to a thorough process of decorative abstraction. A painting such as

Sleeping Girl, exhibited at the gallery of the Barc de Boutteville in November 1892, would surely have impressed Maillol for its purity and decorative design. Although Denis's image is more courageously abstract than Maillol's profile series, his works do point in the direction Maillol will follow.[53] Furthermore Maillol acknowledged Denis's impact on his development: "Maurice Denis had a deep influence on me. Some of my tapestries are a Maurice Denis translated into wool."[54]

According to Nabi theory, the "synthesis" was the single most important way in which a true Symbolist artist could incorporate his visual sensations into a finished work of art:

> For "to synthesize"... is not to simplify in the sense of suppressing certain parts of the object; it is to simplify in the sense of making clear. It is, in sum, to arrange hierarchically, to submit each painting to a single rhythm, to a dominant, to sacrifice, to subordinate, to generalize.[55]

In Maillol's paintings from this time on, one sees the repeated attempt to follow Denis's dictum; to submit each painting to a single dominant rhythm. One can observe in these works the absence of modeling or indications of light. This helps create a clear, well-defined flattened image of the heads. In each painting Maillol suppressed details of clothing, background, physiognomy and locale.

In both *Woman in Mauve* and *Girl with a Black Hat* the solid yellow backdrops, while still present, have been overlaid by a dense wall of foliage which frames the sitters. This more extensive foliage provides a cooler ambiance for the women. In *Girl with a Black Hat,* the shape of the greenery echo the form of the sitter, leaning slightly from right to left.

The importance of Renaissance portraits for the entire series has been noted above. While Maillol could have known a variety of Renaissance portraits through reproductions, he had access to one of Pisanello's finest portraits of this type, the *Portrait of Margherita Gonzaga* (1445-49) in the Louvre.[56] In this painting, the profile of the sitter is defined by a precise, sensitive line. The face becomes a flat plane; there is no modeling. This is precisely the way Maillol builds his profile paintings.

The background of the Pisanello portrait is filled with dark green foliage. Yellow and pink flowers are dotted over this surface. In the group of paintings under discussion Maillol adapts this foliated background as well. The similarities are too consistent to be coincidental. Pisanello's *Portrait of Margherita Gonzaga* is an important source for these, more synthetic paintings.

Girl with a Black Hat can be considered both a finished painting in its own right and a preparatory exercise for the larger-scaled work *Two Girls* (fig. 9). The figure on the left is dressed in white and faces the viewer directly. The right-hand figure is in profile, wearing a purple robe. The latter woman is the same sitter seen in *Girl with a Black Hat,* and in fact, wears the same black hat. The woman in white is the young model of *Girl in Blue* and *Spring* (fig. 7).

Two Girls (fig. 9) is a carefully conceived, well-thought-out, and not particularly subtle allegory. As in *Spring* (fig. 7), Maillol is juxtaposing two opposing archetypes of Woman: the simple virginal country girl and the elegantly dressed, sophisticated city woman. The symbolic interpretations discussed above in connection with *Spring* can be applied with equal validity to this work. The woman on the left confronts the viewer directly with wide open eyes. She stands straightforward and unashamed. By contrast, the right-hand figure in purple is closed off from the viewer; she is fashionably dressed and conveys the impression that she possesses sexual knowledge and experience.

The foliage of the background further emphasizes the contrasts between the two. Behind the virgin, there are softly rounded leaf forms in pale green and yellow. The leaves behind the figure in purple are hard, spiked, and almost tropically exotic. This vegetation, like Maillol's use of trees, provides visual analogies to the personalities of the figures.

The way in which the faces of the two women are painted provides another contrast. The face of the figure on the right is uniformly pale; there is little modeling or indications of cheekbones. Her lips lack color and are barely indicated. Her profile is very sharp, almost chiseled, like the forms of the leaves behind her.

By contrast, the face of the woman on the left has quite a bit of modeling. Her lips are a bright orange color, and a blush spreads across her cheekbones. In sum, her face is depicted much more naturalistically. The ethereal, deadly pallor of the woman in profile is contrasted to the wholesomeness and fully modeled three-dimensionality of the younger woman on the left.

The movement toward replacing the fractured and residually Impressionist brushstroke with broader, simplified areas of pure color, noted above, can be compared to Gauguin's stylistic development, which evolved from the very impressionistic touch of 1888-89 to the clear contours and simplified color planes of the paintings from the first Tahitian voyage (1891-93).

A pastel (Gug. 114) presents the next logical step in this stylistic progression. When Maillol discussed a very similar work[57] with Henri Frère, he said:

> This is a replica.[58] I made another one, which is the best picture I made. She is turned to the other side.... It was splendid. This is the portrait of my mistress, before I married. A girl who made tapestries...[59]

From this information, one may date this work between the summer of 1893 and 1894. One may assume that Maillol would not have had a mistress in the few months of 1895 which preceded his marriage.

In this work, Maillol develops another formal correlation between women and nature. He has used the same pattern of lightly drawn parallel lines to indicate the texture of both the hair of the young woman and the tree trunk. This patterning catches the viewer's eye almost immediately since the image is so starkly simple. One is meant to conclude that there is a similarity in the protective coverings of both the tree and the head of the woman.

In this pastel, one sees all the elements of the profile series, but rendered in an even more simplified way. There are no extraneous details; the contours of the figure's head and shoulders are emphasized; there is no modeling or play of color. Also Maillol has depicted the figure with an expressive gesture of the hand brought to the forehead. Because the face remains composed, romantic sentimentalism or melodrama is avoided. It is a gesture open to varied interpretations, a symbolic movement. In this image, Maillol's style achieves an increased simplicity, and an increased power of expression from the gesture. Perhaps this explains why he considered it to be his best painting.

A possible influence on Maillol's increased simplification of style could be the more mature works of Gauguin, after the Café Volpini show. For example, Maillol would surely have known a profile portrait[60] which Gauguin drew in pastel while Mme. de Monfreid posed for her husband in the latter's studio. The emphasized contour and extreme, almost Japanese simplicity of the Gauguin head is similar to the Maillol work. Even the medium of pastel is the same.

Paintings after 1895

The *Portrait of Mme. Maillol* (fig. 10) marks the inception of a new, exploratory phase of Maillol's painting, where one can note a more varied stylistic pattern influenced by different sources. Over the course of the next few years, the scale, presentation of the female figure, symbolism and style of Maillol's painting move in new directions.

This period of increased experimentation coincides with other changes in Maillol's life: the establishment of the tapestry workshop, the date of his marriage, and the beginning of his activity in sculpture. Indeed, considering these factors it would be surprising if Maillol's painting style did not undergo substantial changes.

The *Portrait of Mme. Maillol* (fig. 10) was painted before Maillol and Clotilde were married in the spring of 1895.[61] A comparison between this work and another earlier version of this portrait[62] (fig. 11) provides insight into Maillol's stylistic development. The earlier version contains the essential compositional elements of the finished portrait; the face of Clotilde viewed in three-quarter, turned towards the right, placed before a dark green background studded with yellow flowers. But the effect of this work differs noticeably from the later, definitive version. First, the figure is positioned to the far left of the picture space and over half of the area is lightly filled in with dark green. This compositional device is not dissimilar to the portrait in Reims (fig. 5) and the Perpignan profile (fig. 6). In this first version (fig. 11), the sitter does not dominate the space at all, but seems almost uncomfortably squeezed to one side. When one compares this to the later portrait (fig. 10) where the figure occupies more than two-thirds of the picture area, the difference in the way in which the subject relates to her world is obvious. Maillol created an image which seems confident and self-assured, unlike the insecure, almost worried earlier presentation. Mme. Maillol displays a Renaissance domination and security within the edges of her portrait. We have already noted Maillol's debt to Renaissance profile portraits; here he merely shifts to a similarly inspired three-quarter view.

One is clearly reminded of Leonardo da Vinci's *Ginevra de' Benci*[63] in which the dark foliated background and dress contrasts with the pale visage, described with perfect linear control. This became a Florentine portrait formula in the third quarter of the fifteenth century, and was used with beautiful results by Ghirlandaio and Lorenzo di Credi, among others.

The method in which the face has been painted is also quite different from the earlier profile series. In the earlier version, the face is a flat, pale beige, with an almost yellow cast. The only indication of modeling is a slight darkening of the intersection of the chin and neck and a light shadow between the eyelid and the brow. There is no cheekbone definition at all. Also the line of the profile from the broadest part of the face, at the cheek to the chin, is an abstract, severe straight line—almost ruler straight. The hair also lacks highlights and is painted in a uniform gray color.

The flat, unmodeled pallor, as well as the compositional formula relates this work to the earlier group of paintings, such as *Woman in Mauve* and *Girl with a Black Hat* discussed above. The second version of the *Portrait of Mme. Maillol* (fig. 10) indicates a desire to create a less severe representation, one with a more forceful presence.

The skin tones in the final portrait are more vibrant and certainly more varied, close in effect to the woman in white (left) in *Two Girls* (fig. 9). The forehead of Mme. Maillol is painted in a warm, beige tone; the cheekbone is made prominent by a shadow in the hollow and is suffused with a pink blush. The mouth, which is outlined in pencil, is brushed in with an orange color. The hair and dress are painted in solid black which, as in *Ginevra de' Benci,* helps to emphasize the warm coloring of the face.

The background has also changed in nature from the earlier works. Here we see a solid, flat dark green surface, enlivened by golden plant-like fronds. The immediate comparison one draws is with the *millefleurs* tapestries of the late Middle Ages which also place their figures against a totally abstract ground of forest green. There is no attempt to create a recognizable, realistic environment. This is different from the earlier works where naturalistic foliage, although it was used non-naturalistically, was the rule, and each scene was brightly lit.

The dark ground, combined with the dark, almost black hair and black dress frame the face, so that the subtleties and modeling in the visage seem to stand out in relief. The darkness surrounding the face brings out, not only the internal modeling, but also the rhythmically curving contour line of her cheekbone which is echoed in the curving golden plants of the background. The gently arched black eyebrows find their counterpoint in the horizontally swelling plant fronds in the lower right corner.

Maillol again turned to the Italian Renaissance, specifically Botticelli, for inspiration in *Two Girls* (fig. 12). This painting shows two women looking towards the left, with necks inclined at just the same angle. The left-hand figure, dressed in a simple blue garment is clearly derived from the figure of Flora in Botticelli's *Primavera*. The wreath of flowers, the hair piled above the crown of the forehead and the crisp linearity of the profiles, all testify to Botticelli's influence.

The woman on the right, however, has an 1890s chignon coiffure and appears to be wearing a contemporary leg-of-mutton sleeved dress. Although there is no attempt here to juxtapose opposing types as we have seen in *Spring* (fig. 7) and *Two Girls* (fig. 9), the figures seem to belong to two different epochs. Perhaps Maillol recognized, in the appearance of his model or in a larger sense, in the spirit of his own personality or culture, an underlying affinity with the Renaissance. In the *döppelganger* effect, he sought to express this affinity across the centuries.

Formally, Maillol's study of the Quattrocento is manifested by the use of more traditional methods of modeling. There is a specific light source, coming from the upper left in this painting, and clearly defined shadows on the necks of the two figures.

It is impossible to determine the space in which these two figures exist. By overlapping them, Maillol seems to want to imply a deeper space than he has used previously. But he denies the existence of that deeper space in several ways. He positions the two women at just the same angle, creating a linear rhythm across the surface. The skin tone is quite similar to the color of the flat yellow background so that the repetition of that color helps to unite the two planes of space. While the figures are overlapping, they appear to be in the same spatial plane. This technique is consistent with Botticelli's *Primavera (Spring)*. Botticelli places all the figures in a shallow foreground plane with minimal overlapping. Therefore, although Maillol does use modeling techniques, he is careful not to create an illusion of three-dimensional space. This would violate too drastically the dictates of avant-garde painting of the period.

While Botticelli's influence in the right-hand figure is clear and undeniable, it does not explain the rather peculiar positioning of these two women. A painting by the English Victorian painter, L. Fairfax Muckley, *The Vestal Virgins Returning to the Temple,* does show two pairs of women positioned in a remarkably similar manner to Maillol's pair. This work was reproduced in an issue of *Studio* in 1894, so Maillol could easily have seen it.

Although Maillol has chosen to use the familiar solid yellow background with gray tree, I believe this painting is more closely related to the *Portrait of Mme. Maillol* (fig. 10) than to *Spring* (fig. 7), because of the Italianate influence and the greater complexity of the image.

A peculiarity of this painting is that both women have their eyes lowered and their gazes directed downwards. The viewer feels compelled to seek for a context outside the confines of the picture space. It is possible that this work is a fragment from a larger canvas.

All the paintings discussed so far have without exception depicted clothed women. Around 1895, Maillol began painting the female nude. This is significant, since the nude is the single formal problem which will dominate his future oeuvre. Maillol could not have been a stranger to the female nude, for a large part of the academic education which he had pursued was devoted to its study. But there are several reasons for the "new" interest in the nude. We know that Maillol had trouble finding models willing to pose nude in Banyuls, because of the strict mores of the town.[64] However, his marriage in 1895 provided him with a permanently available model. As one might suppose, the figure and features of Mme. Maillol appear in his works of this period with great regularity. This also corresponds to the period in which he began to carve nude figures in wood in his spare time. It is possible that the more tangible art of sculpture, which in Western Civilization has been focused on the nude human form, stimulated him to explore the female nude and the depiction of flesh in paint.

Therefore, it seems logical that when his interest focused on painting the nude he would turn to Renoir for inspiration. Renoir was the greatest contemporary painter of the nude—a specialist in the female form. Furthermore, the type of figure which Renoir was painting, a fleshy, full-hipped, voluptuous nude, was just the type which Maillol identified with his Banyuls women and wanted to create in paint and sculpture. Maillol has said: "If I had persisted in painting, I would have remained influenced by Renoir. I made some small paintings which resemble his."[65] Evidence of this interest in Renoir exists in two small paintings, *Bather Seated on White Drapery* (fig. 13), and *Bather.*[66]

Bather Seated on White Drapery shows a nude female poised in an awkward balance on her haunches, with legs severely bent and crossed, hanging unsupported in mid-air. Her right arm is also sharply bent and covering her face. She is placed against a green and gold ambience, and the only true landscape element is the bush near her feet. This figure certainly bears comparison with the bather on the far left in Renoir's *The Large Bathers.*[67] Maillol's figure has the same tilted and unbalanced position. Although the position of the left arm of Maillol's figure is different, the spirit of the work and the compact and voluptuous nude set in a landscape is very similar. Although *The Large Bathers* was exhibited at the Galerie Durand-Ruel in May 1892, there is a possibility that both works share a common source; Michelangelo's *Night* in the Medici Chapel.

Bather shows a figure, again seated on a white drapery (a favorite motif of Renoir's), set in a landscape. The right leg is crossed over the left leg while the left arm reaches to wipe the toe of the opposing foot. This work compares closely with many paintings by Renoir, but especially with numbers 523 and 618 in the Daulte catalogue. The 618 was owned by Henri Lerolle, a great patron of Denis and a friend of all the Nabis.

It is virtually impossible to date these two works by Maillol with any precision. The handling of the paint seems very swift and assured, so it would be unlikely to date from very early in Maillol's career. I believe that they were painted around 1895, when Maillol had reached a crisis in his painting and was searching for a new personal style. The rich blue, green, and gold tones of this work are also evident in other paintings from 1895-96. However, it is not completely impossible, though not likely, that these works were painted under the direct stimulus of meeting the master himself. We know that Maillol modeled Renoir's bust in 1907, and at that time Renoir painted a small panel showing three views of a Maillol statuette (now in the Vierny collection). According to Maillol, this encounter stimulated Renoir to try sculpture himself. However, in 1907, Maillol was very actively pursuing his own career in sculpture and had generally abandoned painting.

The following group of works represent Maillol's fullest exploration of the female nude in painting, and if our supposition is correct would indicate the continued influence of Renoir's female type: *The Wave* (fig. 14), *The Mediterranean* (fig. 15) and *The Woman and the Wave* (fig. 16). Mme. Maillol modeled for all three works which treat the theme of the nude and the ocean.

Maillol told Frère that *The Woman and the Wave* was painted the first year Mme. Maillol came to Paris. Since we know that the newly-married couple arrived in Paris in the spring of 1895 we can establish 1895-96 as a date for these paintings.

The design of *The Wave* is the most strictly derivative and the surface reveals the least skillful application of paint in this group. For these reasons, it seems likely that it is the earliest of the three paintings. The pose of the figure comes directly from Gauguin's painting *Ondine* or *In the Waves.*[68] *Ondine* depicts a female nude with back turned to the viewer; she is submerged in water to the level of the thighs and stands before a wall of water which fills the entire canvas. (She was paired with a crouching figure in *At the Black Rocks*.) With the exception of the sharply bent right arm which he has retained, Maillol has altered the Gauguin pose considerably. In place of the awkward position of Gauguin's figure, with her head thrown back and body stretched diagonally from left to right, Maillol has turned the figure into a much more decorative form. Maillol's woman is centralized in the picture space, the diagnonal movement of the torso towards the left is counterbalanced by the bent upraised right arm and leg. Maillol has substituted a softly curving, voluptuous nude for the sharp boniness of Gauguin's figure.

A likely source for these changes in the figure's position, which would explain both the fleshiness of the figure and its more graceful position, is the figure on the left in Renoir's *Large Bathers*.[69] Although Maillol's figure is not bent as sharply as Renoir's the disposition of the visible arm and leg are quite close. Thus Maillol manages to synthesize Gauguin's conception with Renoir's more pleasing form to create an original work of art.

The body of the figure in *The Wave* is painted in an impasto: the tone of the skin is an unmodeled solid beige. The way in which the paint is applied is clearly reminiscent of earlier works such as *Woman in Mauve*, where the paleness of the face sits on the surface as a flat plane.

Maillol repeated the design in a ceramic bas-relief[70] as well as in a woodcut.[71] This seems to be the earliest example of a practice Maillol would repeat often in the next ten years: adapting a motif originated in one medium into a second and even third work in different media. His last executed tapestry *The Bather* (fig. 27) is a further variation on this motif. *The Bather* combines the drapery held in the figure's left hand in *The Woman and the Wave* (fig. 16) with the bent knee and submersion in the water of *The Wave* (fig. 14).

To understand the meaning of the painting, however, one must return to *At the Black Rocks*. Although Maillol's image lacks the specific contrast of female types, his figure (along with the woman of *The Woman and the Wave*) implies some of the same ideas as Gauguin's image—openness to natural forces, acceptance of sexuality, a unity between the natural forces of the seas and the life-force within the female. One is not dealing with an anecdotal depiction of women playing in the water, but rather an iconic image of Woman linked with the ocean, submerging her individual identity (this would explain the hidden face) to strive towards a synthesis with nature. The female depicted is not meant to indicate one specific woman, but is an archetypal symbol representing all women. It cannot be coincidental that this symbolic image of woman, who carries life within her body floating in water, is merged in this image with the sea, the source from which all life began.

La Côte d'Azur or *The Mediterranean* (fig. 15) is the most complex and monumental expression of this theme. The painting depicts a voluptuous, robust nude standing on the edge of the sea facing the viewer. Above her right shoulder, she holds a white drapery which billows outwards and is caught with her left hand. A blue piece of material lies on the ground to one side, as if recently discarded. The verticality of her body is echoed by two young trees, one of which partly obscures the figure. The shape of the coastline is clearly indicated. It forms an arc sweeping around the left-hand side of the painting, suggesting the bay of Banyuls. A tree closes off the painting on the left while the dark blue of the sea extends outward on the right, interrupted by two rocky mounds around which the sea churns. The colors used in this work, as in the other two paintings, have darkened into richly saturated tones; no longer are the bright yellows and pale pastels of his earlier painting evident. Bernard Dorival has described this painting in the following way:

> Dark blues and jade greens dominate the dark and saturated color, and light tones are so completely banished that Maillol gives to the embodiments of his women a gray or bright tint which is not without analogy to the flesh of Gauguin and Vuillard. Arranged flatly, smoothly, without half-tones, this color seeks to stress the impression that we are before a painting and that the painted work is not a copy of nature but an exercise of submission to the laws of painting. . . .
>
> . . . . the curves of the second plane are opposed to the upright verticals of the first, but the antithesis is not shocking since Maillol takes care to inflate, to incline, to curve these verticals a bit. And it is marvelous to note the equilibrium of this work which the placement of a standing figure might have imbalanced; Maillol has arranged the light and dark tones in such a happy way that rhythm and harmony are created.[72]

One is also reminded quite strongly of Botticelli's voluptuous Venus born from the sea, with her long flowing hair. A more contemporary prototype for the painting is Gauguin's *Te Nave Nave Fenua* (dated 1892) or *Fragrant Earth*.[73] This work presents a large-scaled female nude placed in the foreground, very close to the viewer, set before a lush background. In both works, one is meant to relate the nude to the landscape. In *Fragrant Earth*, we are presented with a "Tahitian Eve before her fall . . . who exudes the same appeal as the wilderness of nature which is her home."[74] *The Mediterranean* reveals a formal connection in the curves of the female body and the Bay of Banyuls behind her. We are meant to see this woman as a visual metaphor for the beauty and fertility of Nature. As a sculptor, Maillol will personify the Mediterranean Sea, the Ile de France, and mountains and rivers exclusively through the female nude. In this painting, Maillol provides the viewer with more information to perceive his meaning. He understands Woman as a creature inextricably linked to organic nature; trees, flowers, oceans and sky, and as a personification of these phenomena.

The connections between women and water illustrated in these paintings will be seen again in the decorative motifs of the ceramic fountains which

Maillol created a few years later (figs. 32 and 33). It also recalls the relief, *La Source* (1896) (fig. 34), where the deep folds of drapery are indistinguishable from falling water.

The general, symbolic meaning of this group of images linking women and water has been discussed in connection with *The Wave* (fig. 14). However, in this particular painting I believe that the female figure is more specifically meant to symbolize the classical spirit of the Mediterranean Sea. The billowing drapery, which echoes the exaggerated swell of the figure's hip, recalls the drapery of certain figures in the art of antiquity. For example, one can see these rounded, full draperies in the famous fresco cycle of the Villa of the Mysteries. Similar drapery appears on vase paintings which also depict the Dionysian Ceremonies and on a relief which decorated the base of a round altar. Both of the works were engraved and published in *Les Monuments antiques du Musée Napoléon,* by Thomas Piroli, Paris, 1804.[75] Maillol would certainly have had access to these or similar works at the Louvre, as well as books of this type.

The punctuation of the picture by upright trees is a typical Nabi device derived from Puvis, which is used by Sérusier in *Incantation* as well as by Denis in several works of 1893, such as *Procession under the Trees* and *The Muses.* Denis's *Grove of the Wise Virgins,* exhibited at the Salon des Indépendants in 1893, provides the closest analogy. In this image, the main figure is framed by two pairs of thin trees, one of which is placed in front of the figure and obscures part of her form.

The formula which Maillol has used to indicate waves is adapted from Gauguin's very linear formula for waves, which was, in turn, inspired by the Japanese treatment of water patterns in woodcuts. We know that Maillol himself owned a Gauguin seascape, *The Beach at Pouldu* (1889).[76] In this painting the foam of the waves is painted in bright white lines which stand out very clearly from the dark green of the sea and the black spots of rocks.[77]

There is a related zincograph of a very similar subject.[78] It shows two women, one facing the viewer with arms raised toward the sun, and the other turned away from the viewer and about to enter the water. The woman positioned frontally is definitely Mme. Maillol, again, the same body which is represented in *The Mediterranean* (fig. 15). In this print, Maillol again used the motif of a young tree to define the foreground space.

In *The Woman and the Wave* (fig. 16), the third painting of this group, Maillol has utilized the familiar profile format of his earlier works. Here, however, the effect is quite dissimilar. Maillol is emphasizing the sensuality of the body. The skin tones are warm and variegated, the cheek is suffused with a blush of pink. Maillol's *Woman and the Wave* is closely related to Courbet's *Woman in the Waves* (1868) in both the subject and composition, as well as a strongly defined sensuality.[79] This strong element of physical presence was not lost on Monfreid who hung Maillol's painting among the Gauguins in his collection.[80]

Henri Frère has recorded Maillol's comments on this painting:

> This is one of my best paintings. My wife was the model, the first year we came to Paris. She had striking breasts, a pretty stomach, very soft. She gave me that. Her hair was not like that. I made her hair more red in order to make a warmer tone. I wanted to make a flesh tone like Gauguin's. The drapery, by contrast, should have been much whiter. It was a great effect of white.[81]

Maillol's goal for his painting would seem to be the creation of a sensuous, almost provocative female, who exudes warmth from her body and her hair. As noted above, he has achieved this quite beautifully. It is interesting that, even at this advanced stage of his painting career, he continued to work with Gauguin's paintings clearly in mind. He also showed a sensitivity to the emotive effects of color and the importance of contrast. The wave is painted in a very abstract formula; concentric circles of royal blue, forest green, chartreuse, and the white of the foam which intermingles with the white drapery encircling her head.

Another painting by Maillol which will be referred to as *Two Bathers* (fig. 17) combines Maillol's newly-found interest in the nude form with his more typical landscape, rather than ocean setting. The painting shows two views of the same figure, one in profile and one from behind, set in a lush pale green landscape, near a small pond and flowering bushes. The figures are framed and separated by thin straight trees. This painting shares several characteristics with *The Mediterranean* (fig. 15). The presence of nudes in the foreground, set against a vast landscape, and the use of trees to divide and accent the picture space, complete with a similar branch of leaves traceable directly to Gauguin which arches over the head of one figure, are aspects found in both works.

The use of the same figure in two different poses is found in paintings Maillol would surely have known. It is used in Puvis's *Women by the Sea,* and Denis's *Triple portrait of Marthe fiancée* and *Soir trinitaire.*

A rather strange aspect of this painting is the color tonalities which are much brighter than Maillol had been using in paintings such as *The Wave* (fig. 14). The green and golds resemble the colors of the plant dyes used in his tapestries, rather than his usual palette, and undoubtedly derive from that experience.

In *The Wave, The Mediterranean* and *Two Bathers* there are no visible parallel brush strokes. Maillol had by now cleanly made his break with Impressionism, even the late and modified post-impressionist touch of Gauguin and Cézanne. His colors are applied smoothly and evenly, with no visible brushstrokes.

This painting differs from Maillol's other two-figure compositions in the use of a back view combined with a profile. Thus, neither figure relates directly to the viewer. However, as in *Spring,* the figure on the right is in profile, and here the implied movement out of the picture space of the woman in the earlier work is made explicit in the striding pose of this nude.

Two other works, dated around 1896, show Maillol working in a very different painting style. *The Washerwomen* (fig. 18) and *Head of a Child* are both executed in a broken series of large rounded dots of colors. We know that the bronze statuette, the *Washerwoman* (Gug. 21), dates from the year 1896. As Maillol almost always originated his ideas for sculpture from two dimensional works, one can assume that the painting dates from this time also. This is the year in which his son, Lucien, was born, which would have provided the impetus for the *Portrait*.

Actually the coexistence of two different styles is not as unlikely as one might think at first, when one compares these two paintings to Maillol's contemporary tapestry cartoons. The technique of *The Washerwomen* is actually very similar to certain of Maillol's cartoons, such as *The Swing*. In these years, 1896-89, Maillol was still very much involved in tapestry production. And, in the case of these two works, he merely uses a painting shorthand for a light, genre subject which he found inappropriate for a "serious," consciously synthetic painting such as *The Mediterranean*. This technique is related to Vuillard's contemporary style.

A set of images painted directly on the walls of a Salon in a private home in Banyuls provides evidence of Maillol's interest in mural decoration, during this period—a previously unknown facet of his activity (fig. 19). The cycle was commissioned by the owners of the house, and consists of five separate pictures of standing women, about three feet tall, dispersed about the four walls of the Salon, dressed in contemporary fashion.[82]

This series was not the first time that Maillol had attempted mural painting: one recalls the theatrical decorations he painted in Paris. However, this is the only surviving example of Maillol's painting which does not fall into the general category of an easel painting. Maillol's willingness to explore other possibilities in painting reflects the contemporary Nabi interest in painting as a decorative art and is closely linked to his concurrent activity in tapestry-making. Furthermore, fresco is the most characteristic painting medium of the Italian Renaissance, the epoch to which Maillol turned for inspiration at this time.

The painting located above the fireplace shows two women standing very close together (fig. 19). Their positions are quite similar to the two figures in the foreground of a tapestry cartoon now in the Vierny collection. The figure on the left clasps a fold in her skirt, a motif encountered in the tapestry *The Enchanted Garden* (fig. 22) as well as in an early statuette, *Clothed Nabi* (Gug. 19). The women are situated, as might be expected, next to a tree, against a landscape background of green and gold; a color scheme encountered in the *Portrait of Mme. Maillol*. All the works, cited above, which share affinities with the frescoes are dated between 1894 and 1896.

The remaining four parts of the cycle are painted in a monochrome. The women themselves have the appearance of painted sculpture: they are colored olive green, reminiscent of bronze, with highlights in gold, and shadows painted in a darker green. Furthermore, they stand on rectangular bases, another sculptural concept, which gives the impression of a lawn or meadow through a regular system of parallel lines used to indicate grass and an uneven, bumpy upper contour.

In fact, these monochromatic women resemble more closely a series of statuettes Maillol sculpted about 1896 than any paintings. The proportions are also quite similar. This correspondence, combined with the similarities in the painting over the fireplace with works created between 1894 and 1896, would strongly suggest 1896-97 as a likely date for the execution of the series. These images are an isolated example in Maillol's career of sculpture influencing painting. Usually, Maillol invented an image in a two-dimensional medium and then transformed it into a piece of sculpture.

The women stand out clearly against the white walls. At most points the outlines of the form are confined by a thin line of darker green. The dresses vary in style from a very slender tubular skirt to a full skirt with deep folds swirling in a graceful arabesque.

Three of these monochromatic images display single women, two positioned frontally, and one in profile. They are carrying in turn, two jugs of wine, two very large feathery cocks, a basket overflowing with produce and another cock. The remaining image shows two women in three-quarter view both bearing baskets filled with ripe, picked grapes accompanied by two small children.

The cycle describes an allegory of the natural productivity of Banyuls. Vineyards are the major agricultural resource of the area (Banyuls is famous in France for its very rich, red wine.) Poultry is commonly bred throughout southern France. The presence of the children would link the fertility of the soil to female fertility.

We have already noted that the women are standing firmly on mounds of earth. Grasses, grape vines and leafy plants spring individually from these plots of earth on either side of the figures, counterbalancing the verticality of the women and providing an additional iconographic reference to the fruits of the earth, the vegetal produce of the region.

The use of women with attributes to convey an allegorical meaning is a fairly common and traditional motif. Many examples can be found in Salon painting and popular imagery. For example in the March 3, 1890 issue of *Illustration* a work by Victor Gilbert entitled *Le Jeune plant* was reproduced. It shows a young, healthy farm girl holding a watering can over a row of new plants. The obvious conclusion is that the title refers as much to this female specimen as to the vegetation beneath her feet. In another issue of *Illustration* (the Christmas issue of 1895) two watercolors by a Mme. Jeanne Borde-Guyon are reproduced. One is entitled *Fleur d'Alsace* the other *Fleur de Russie*. Particularly in the latter painting, we see the profile, bust-length image so common in Maillol's paintings. But aside from compositional similarities, the idea of using a female figure to personify a geographical area or more broadly, a natural phenomenon is rather similar to the conception of Maillol's fresco cycle.

Taken as a group, this mural cycle provides us with an insight into the way Maillol handles more traditional imagery and his ability to evolve a satisfying decorative mural program. They also testify to Maillol's increasing involvement with sculpture, so much so that his vision is now dominated by his activity in that medium. Gone are all traces of Puvis's frieze-like compositions. Here, the figures are isolated, discrete units, like individual statuettes.

It is fitting to conclude this chronology of Maillol's painting with a series which reveals a sculptor's vision. In this way, the cycle points directly to Maillol's future which will be devoted so completely to the making of beautiful works of sculpture.

Maillol's paintings can be divided broadly into three periods. The earliest and most derivative group, which dates from 1889 to 1891, includes the copies of Puvis de Chavannes's compositions and the series of Gauguinesque landscapes. Maillol is following the models of quite well-established contemporary figures and has not yet found a personal style.

Most of Maillol's paintings in the second period, from 1891 to 1895, are bust-length heads set in profile. He is now looking to a wider variety of sources for inspiration both within and beyond his immediate artistic milieu. With these paintings, Maillol is establishing an individual synthetic-Symbolist idiom to express a chaste image of womanhood.

However, the restrictions which he imposed upon himself for the extremely simplified profile images proved too confining. The paintings after 1895, which form the third and final group, demonstrate Maillol's desire for a more complex iconography. The nude female form appears in Maillol's painted oeuvre only at this time. Renoir is a significant influence in these works, which reveal as well the continued importance of Gauguin for Maillol's vision.

These paintings, taken as a group, testify to Maillol's desire to create a personal statement. However, he never seems quite able to evolve a truly original body of works. He appears constantly to be following the way marked by one or another contemporary, rather than leading his generation, like Gauguin, Cézanne, or even Denis in this period. While Maillol's paintings open no new paths, they are pleasing, technically proficient works which do have grace and charm and interesting subjects.

Painting occupied less and less of his time and energy after 1895. By 1897 or 1898, he was no longer painting; his energies were directed toward ceramics, sculpture and tapestry-making. The reasons why Maillol stopped painting may never be fully known, but Maillol himself must have realized the limitations of his talents as a painter. Recognizing that he was not among the best painters, he sought another way to make his reputation as an artist. Also, Maillol loved working with his hands and believed that artists should be craftsmen, involved in the manual labor necessary to produce the art object. In this respect, his instinctive ideas are related to the ideology of the British Arts and Crafts Movement. Maillol's respect for craftsmanship and his regrets over the loss of fine workmanship in France run through his biography. Painting, which involved so little direct manipulation of materials, may simply have been less pleasurable to him than the modeling of a statue or working with yarns for his tapestries.[83] Here is a persuasive explanation for Maillol's ultimate rejection of painting as his proper sphere. As will be shown, the full range of his talent only found expression in these more tangible media.

However, the years he spent as a painter were certainly not wasted ones. The impact of his trained painter's eye will be thoroughly demonstrated in the form of his sculpture and in his tapestries. Also, Maillol's conceptual approach to art was conditioned by these years in the Symbolist avant-garde milieu. A thorough understanding of the paintings establishes the proper framework for an accurate interpretation of all Maillol's subsequent images of women.

Therefore, from the secure base which a knowledge of the paintings provides, one may more safely proceed toward an examination of the tapestries. With an analysis of the sculpture from the 1890s, the picture of Maillol's formative decade will be complete.

3

The Tapestries

For approximately seven years, a considerable portion of Maillol's energies was devoted to the art of tapestry-making. Maillol returned to Banyuls during the summer of 1893 for his annual visit. That year he set up a tapestry workshop with five or six local girls as workers.[1] He exhibited his first tapestry (or an *Essai de tapisserie*, as it was listed in the catalogue) in 1893, at the Salon of the Société Nationale des Beaux Arts. His last completed work, *The Bather* (fig. 27), was created before 1900.

All the executed tapestries except *The Bather* depict between four and seven women in contemporary dress. Very limited activity is indicated; women stand or sit, sometimes listening to a book being read or playing musical instruments. Most figures do nothing. These gatherings are always set in gardens.

Maillol's interest extended to every phase of tapestry production. With characteristic thoroughness, and attention to craftsmanship, he applied himself with energy and determination to the technical problems of the medium. He created the designs, and closely supervised their execution in wools he had personally selected and dyed.

Actually, "tapestry" is an incorrect term for Maillol's creations, since true tapestries are woven on a loom. Colored yarns are threaded between tautly strung wool cords. Since Maillol could not afford a loom during these active years, all his completed tapestries are executed in a flat stitch, petit-point technique in which the needle is passed over and under the support material. The stitches are usually about one centimeter long.

Maillol knew that the tapestry industry of his time had lost direction. He said: "Today, no one knows how to dye or spin; the French Revolution cut the necks of most of the artisans."[2] At this time, the Gobelins factory was producing transcriptions of paintings in wool. Maillol wanted to penetrate the special nature of tapestries, to create designs specifically for the medium, returning the art to one true to its own requirements. He sought to restore tapestry to the position of dominance among the arts which it held during the Middle Ages.

Tapestry is not a particularly rigid medium; it can be manipulated to produce a variety of desired effects. Maillol's images, as well as exploiting patterns which showed the wools to advantage, satisfied the requirements for a true Symbolist work of art, as understood in the period: flatness, the use of elements of reality to create a mysterious or symbolic image, and simplicity or synthesis in the description of the forms. These tapestries are unquestionably the most beautiful and most interesting products to emerge from the spate of activity in the medium in the 1890s. They have been termed the most significant French tapestries of their period and century.[3]

Before beginning an analysis of Maillol's tapestries, one should understand the context in which they were created. His efforts in this medium were certainly not isolated attempts, divorced from the artistic climate of his times. There was a proliferation of tapestry-making activity around 1890. Humbert attributes this revived interest in France to a conjunction of similar formal aspects in the Nabi paintings and in late medieval tapestries: e.g. simplification of line, economy of colors, flat tones and the use of symbols.[4]

In addition to these formal concerns, tapestries possess certain qualities which coincide with two other avant-garde interests of this time. The Nabis considered easel painting to be an inferior genre. They wished to create monumental works of art, i.e. wall decorations. Jan Verkade describes this attitude most clearly in his autobiography:

> Toward the beginning of 1890, a war cry was launched from one studio to another: "No more easel paintings! Down with useless objects! Painting cannot usurp a liberty which isolates it from other arts. The painter's work begins where that of the architect ends. Walls to decorate! Down with perspective! The wall must remain a surface, it must not be pierced by the representation of infinite horizons. There are no pictures, there are only decorations!"[5]

All the members of the Nabis painted decorative mural cycles during the 1890s.

As well as trying to expand the role and size of paintings, the Nabis were also interested in breaking down the divisions within the arts:

> The merit of the Nabi movement lies in its having been conscious, from its origin, of the new possibilities and in its suppression of divisions which too narrowly limit the diverse forms of art; the Nabi did not want to be exclusively a painter, but an artist . . . "[6]

Again, it is clear that Maillol's concerns coincided with those of the Nabis. Maillol considered himself to be an artisan, a craftsman rather than a specialist in any particular medium.

The Nabi interest in the decorative arts, and possibly Maillol's as well, can be traced directly back to Gauguin and Bernard, who never confined themselves exclusively to painting. Gauguin began working in ceramics in 1886 and carving wood reliefs in 1889. His interest in the decorative arts was not a superficial or passing one. He wrote to Daniel de Monfreid in August 1892: "Understand that I was born to make an art industry and I can only end with this. Be it stained glass, furniture, ceramics, etc., these are fundamentally my aptitudes much more than actual painting."[7]

Prior to his departure for Egypt, in 1893, Emile Bernard created a series of tapestries, or rather embroideries. It is logical to consider these works in wool as simply another aspect of Bernard's fascination with the decorative arts. During the period of his association with Gauguin, he carved the wooden door panels of two armoires and designed stained glass windows, as well as making paintings, drawings, and lithographs, in addition to the tapestries. One perfect integration of these two Nabi-Synthetist interests, i.e., wall decoration and the exploration of media other than painting, is the art of the tapestry.

Although the Pont Aven circle's interest in the decorative arts was undoubtedly a very important influence on Maillol, Gauguin was not the first artist of the century to explore new designs and techniques in the decorative arts. That role clearly belongs to William Morris. Beginning in the 1860s, Morris and a group of associates (most notably Walter Crane and Edward Burne-Jones) began designing textile and wallpaper patterns, furniture, stained glass and, most importantly for Maillol's development, tapestries. Morris's interest, specifically, in tapestries dates from 1878.[8] In 1881, *The Goose Girl,* the first large-scale figural tapestry, was woven under Morris's supervision—after a cartoon by Walter Crane. Later, in 1890-91, Morris entrusted the designs for a tapestry series based upon Malory's *Legend of the Holy Grail* to Edward Burne-Jones. The first executed tapestry of this series was the *Adoration* (1890).

It is highly probable that Maillol was aware of this revival of tapestry-making in England. (According to Jacques Lethève, the English review *Studio* was widely circulated in France, after 1893.[9] This magazine would have kept the French well informed of the latest developments in the revival of the decorative arts by the Arts and Crafts movement.) However, there is no documentary evidence which suggests that Maillol actually saw any of these tapestries before 1900, when the *Adoration* was displayed at the Universal Exposition, in Paris. However, certain aspects of the Merton Abbey tapestries are quite relevant to Maillol's works. Often women are used exlusively or far outnumber men; the backgrounds are usually heavily foliated gardens; the figures are not individualized and are usually arranged in the foreground plane; and decorative plant borders are used. All these factors are characteristic of Maillol's compositions, which seem to indicate that he was familiar with the Merton Abbey tapestries, if only through black and white illustrations in *Studio.*

Despite these stylistic similarities, Maillol's works are a conscious turning from the medievalizing religious, historical, or allegorical subjects which

Morris and Burne-Jones favored. His tapestries strive for a simplicity and intimacy, quite different from tapestries such as the ornate, detailed compositions of the *Adoration,* with its traditional Christian iconography.

It is tempting to suppose that Maillol was exposed to the catalogue of the first Arts and Crafts Exhibition, of 1888, in which Morris discussed tapestry:

> The noblest of the weaving arts is Tapestry in which there is nothing mechanical: it may be looked upon as a mosaic of pieces of colour made up of dyed threads and is capable of producing wall ornament of any degree of elaboration within the proper limits of duly considered decorative work.
>
> As in all wall decoration, the first thing to be considered in the designing of Tapestry is the force, purity, and elegance of the silhouette of the objects represented, and nothing vague or indeterminate is admissible. But special excellence can be expected from it. Depth of tone, richness of colour, and exquisite gradation of tints are easily to be obtained in Tapestry; and it also demands that crispness and abundance of beautiful detail which was the especial characteristic of fully developed Medieval Art.[10]

Each point Morris makes is directly relevant to Maillol's tapestries. Morris emphasizes that tapestry is a totally nonmechanical method of creating wall decoration. This would have appealed to Maillol, who was very concerned with aspects of hand craftsmanship. Morris stresses the silhouette of the figures as a most important factor in the tapestry. Maillol's sensitivity to this factor will be demonstrated in the tapestries themselves and documented by the preparatory drawings. Maillol's concern with the creation of his own plant dyes indicates his desire to achieve the "richness of color" Morris mentions. Easily obtainable "gradations of tints" follows from the artist's direct control of the dyeing process. Finally Maillol's tapestries are enriched with "an abundance of beautiful detail"; flower, foliage, and drapery enliven every part of the composition with rich and intricate patterns. Therefore, although the subjects of Maillol's tapestries differ from those produced in the Morris circle, the theoretical basis and certain principles of composition are firmly linked to the Arts and Crafts movement.

Although it cannot be proven that Maillol had read Morris's text, he was certainly aware of the chapter on tapestry in Charles Blanc's *Grammaire des arts décoratifs* (published in 1882), in which the author discusses the properties of a variety of media.

Blanc establishes the basic principles of tapestry and then provides a series of guidelines for the tapestry-maker concerning principles of composition, arrangement of colors, and choice of subjects. Since Blanc's earlier work, *Grammaire des arts du dessin,* was a standard artists' handbook used by the Postimpressionists as well as more conservative artists, Maillol would naturally have referred to this text for guidance.[11]

In contrast to the Gobelins, Blanc understands that a tapestry has its own nature, distinct from paintings. He stresses the fact that tapestries are decorative. They mask the nudity of the wall but should not try to disguise the fact that they cover a flat surface, since the inhabitant must feel enclosed and protected by the wall, for which the tapestry is only a covering.[12] To this end, tapestries should have a high horizon line to suppress the effects of perspective and limit the amount of area of the tapestry devoted to sky.

According to Blanc, all the figures should appear to be on approximately the same plane, close to the viewer. As will be seen, Maillol usually positions his figures in the foreground and the horizon line is quite high.

Blanc maintains that black and white show up poorly because of the uneven surface of the tapestry. Therefore, the designer should not try to achieve the delicate tonal effects which can be carried off on the smooth, flat surface of a painting. His colors should be clear and bright; half tones should be avoided. Since all the figures should be placed close to the viewer, the intensity of colors would seem quite natural. Maillol's tapestries avoid tonal contrasts assiduously, using just those pure colors Blanc recommends, occasionally graduated in intensity.

Maillol was very conscious of the importance of the distribution of the colors in his tapestries. He described one of the principles which guided him: "It is necessary that all is coordinated from top to bottom.... If you have a blue up high, one needs a blue at the bottom.... When a tapestry looks gray in the photo, it is always very good. What is not good are large contrasts."[13] These comments relate to ways of maintaining the decorative flatness of a tapestry. An even distribution of colors of similar intensity would emphasize the surface in each portion of the composition. Keeping value relationships fairly close would also knit the surface together—no one part, lighter or darker, could dominate the composition, thus throwing the other parts into relief.

Blanc then addresses himself to the types of subjects which are most appropriate to tapestries. He rejects subjects which belong to history painting. In his opinion, genre scenes lose their charm when enlarged, appearing "revoltingly vulgar." Looking back over the history of tapestry, Blanc sees that most subjects were inspired by "poetry and fantasy."[14] The tapestry designer can invent his own subjects since man's powers of imagination are the most readily stimulated when he is confined to his home and in familiar surroundings where his fancies may wander. Therefore, the tapestry designer need not render facts or depict objects too naturalistically. Blanc is permitting the tapestry designer a freedom of invention, much broader than the painter's or sculptor's. He concludes his essay:

> How long would this life seem, which one says is too short, if it were dedicated to the prose of reality, if art were not there to lead us into *the enchanted gardens* of the ideal world!...[author's italics]
>   The imagination plays its part there: it desires forms and colors which encourage peregrinations of revery; even though it permits imitation of nature, it wishes that reality appears only as a state of memory and that it be transposed into the realm of dreams."[15]

It is precisely these "Enchanted Gardens" (the title of one of Maillol's tapestries) which Maillol has chosen to represent in his works. His images avoid the prosaic, the description of scenes from daily life, and provide the jumping-off point for the imagination. Maillol's works so precisely reflect Blanc's ideas on tapestry that one may assume that he studied this text, using it as a resource for his personal conception of the medium.[16]

However, Blanc's essay could not help Maillol in his search for visual models to achieve these goals. One source for the form of Maillol's tapestries is Emile Bernard's embroidery, *Women Picking Pears at Pont Aven* (1888),[17] which shows two women in a stylized landscape (fig. 20).[18]

This work would surely have captured Maillol's attention. One sees here, in a more primitive form, all the basic components of Maillol's tapestries; female figures dressed in contemporary costume, a landscape setting, avoidance of traditional perspective techniques, limitation of the number of colors and very limited action. These elements had already appeared in Maillol's paintings and would be fully exploited in his tapestries. Both Bernard's and Maillol's tapestries are executed in a similar system of parallel flat stitches.[19]

Although there is no hard evidence to prove that Maillol saw Bernard's tapestry, his proximity to Gauguin in 1890 and 1891, and the latter's still close association with Bernard during these years, encourages such a supposition. Denis confirms this, in a round-about way: "The terra cottas and sculpted woods of the Master of Tahiti [Gauguin] as well as the tapestry cartoons of Emile Bernard were not without influence on his formation."[20]

During the 1890s, Paul Ranson, one of the original Nabis, and his wife were also involved in tapestry-making. To determine whether his works could have been a direct stimulus for Maillol's activity, it would be necessary to establish more precise dates for his cartoons.[21] Although Ranson's tapestries both technically and stylistically, offer more points of contrast than similarity to those of Maillol, his activity in the medium is significant because he is a contemporary linked with the same avant-garde circle and the duration of his activity coincides with Maillol's.

Women in White[22] was executed by Mme. Ranson in 1894-95. Possibly, the cartoon dates from a few years earlier.[23] Sweeping linear arabesques define the form. The Art Nouveau design of this work differs markedly from Maillol's characteristically stiffer, more controlled images, although there are traces of Art Nouveau patterns in Maillol's early tapestries. Ranson was part of the original Nabis from the Atelier Julian, but his style was the most impregnated by the linear sinuousity of Art Nouveau.

In the executed tapestry which I was able to inspect, the wools were extremely thick. The stitching followed the contour of the outline of the figure; portions within these outlines were executed in a half cross-stitch; the stitches weave in an interlocking manner. This contrasts markedly with the flat stitching on Maillol's tapestries, described above. Maillol's technique, therefore, is much closer to that of Bernard than to Ranson.

However, according to Maillol, the main stimulus to create tapestries came directly from the medieval tapestries on display at the Musée de Cluny, which he studied at length.[24] Maillol told Cladel: "Today, a gothic tapestry gives me more pleasure than a Cézanne."[25] To understand this accolade, one should know that, to Maillol, Cézanne was "the greatest painter of our epoch."[26] Certainly, by comparison with the Gobelins tapestries of the seventeenth, eighteenth, and nineteenth centuries, the Cluny tapestries would have awakened a feeling for the possibilities of the medium. It is not surprising that Maillol should interest himself in works of art produced during an earlier epoch. In order to break out of the heritage of renaissance illusionism many young artists in the 1890s were studying works from a wide variety of periods and cultures. Denis mentions Greek metopes, Byzantine mosaics and medieval art as examples of the great decorative tradition which artists should try to emulate in order to restore painting to its former nobility.[27] Of course, Gauguin's interest in more primitive art forms such as the Javanese reliefs of Borobudur, medieval Breton sculpture and Egyptian tomb paintings is documented by the undisguised appearance of these models in his paintings.

At that time, the major tapestry cycles, *La Dame à licorne* and *La Vie seigneuriale* were already on display at Cluny.[28] Particularly in the latter series one sees many points of comparison with Maillol's images. In several episodes of the cycle, *The Bath* and *Embroidery,* only women are depicted, occupied in very quiet, intimate tasks. The figures are placed against a *millefleurs* background in a way quite similar to Maillol's division of his tapestries and paintings into a figural plane and a landscape backdrop.

In these medieval examples there is a reduction of detail so that each element becomes important. The contours of the women stand out very clearly against the dark green ground. There is an elegance of form and sense of timelessness which Maillol has managed to capture in his own tapestries.

However, one will search in vain for evidence of direct quotations from medieval tapestries in Maillol's works. He was not copying medieval examples. He used contemporary costumes and hair fashions for his figures, often providing them with a plausible activity to explain their presence in the scene. The women are set in possible landscapes rather than the *millefleurs* backgrounds of the medieval works. In sum, Maillol's tapestries present images which are as much a reflection of his own age as the medieval tapestries were of theirs.

Blanc, as noted above, urged the tapestry-maker to create fantasy worlds; in his term, "enchanted gardens." Maillol took him literally, it appears, and the garden setting is a constantly recurring motif in almost all Maillol's tapestries. The garden setting is rich with associations accumulated over a long history of use in literature and the visual arts. While it is impossible to trace here all the complexities of the motif, I would like to suggest a few of its associations. The garden came to be thought of as a setting for love in Greek literature. By Roman times, the association of a *locus amoenus,* literally a lovely place, or pleasance, as the setting for the gods of love is firmly fixed.[29] During the Middle Ages the garden setting retained its associations with the gods of earthly love and became identified as the proper setting for lovers. Many murals and tapestries linked with marriages feature garden settings.

Furthermore, the garden is associated with the earthly paradise, derived from the Biblical Garden of Eden, the perfect setting for an idealized vision of the world. (The enclosed garden, the *hortus conclusus,* also becomes a recurring symbol of the Virgin Mary. The Virgin is often shown in a lovely, shaded, green garden, seated on the ground as the "Madonna of Humility," but Maillol was less interested in such overtly Christian connotations.)

Maillol would have understood the association of the garden as the setting for lovers from the *millefleurs* tapestries at Cluny. There are several scenes of courtly love in the series *La Vie seigneurial.* Another tapestry at Cluny, *Scene of Love,* shows a courting couple. The woman is seated on the ground, while the man advances holding a red heart in his hand.

The medieval *millefleurs* backgrounds would seem to imply, in modern terms, an outdoor setting, but a cultivated or civilized ambience. Maillol translates that into a contemporary equivalent, the garden. Although Maillol's gardens are populated only with women, and show no overt scenes of love, the sense of the garden as the place where lovers can dream, a place set apart from the cares and activities of the "real" world is a quality which he has retained. Van Marle, in his discussion of the "Garden of Love" stresses the allegorical nature of the locale. He defines the garden as "a sort of land of dreams and love, with an abstract significance."[30] This description expresses the quality of remoteness and untouchability of Maillol's gardens. Maillol's women do seem to be in a dream-like zone, somewhere outside of the viewer's experiential world. This, of course, was precisely his intention. Furthermore, the motif of music-making, which Maillol incorporated in two later tapestries, is closely associated with the *locus amoenus.*

However, neither Bernard's tapestries nor the Cluny works fully explain the appearance of Maillol's tapestries. There are other sources which, I believe, must have influenced the design of these works. One source for these images is contemporary fashion plates. In fashion magazines, double page illustrations were often devoted to a tableau of women, lined up one next to the other in a frieze-like arrangement, set against a garden landscape, showing off the latest dress styles. Fairly often in these magazines one sees two women viewed from the front or the back with heads bent together in conversation. This specific motif is used by Maillol for the pair of figures in the foreground of *The*

Enchanted Garden (fig. 22). A drawing which is a design for a tapestry documents Maillol's interest in the fashion plate. At least ten figures are ranged across the page, posed to show off their dresses.[31]

Gardens and parks are used frequently by all the Nabi painters. Although Vuillard generally preferred interior settings for his works, the six panel mural cycle for Alexandre Natanson (1894) is set in a park; the figures are placed against a background of greenery. Bonnard's *Croquet Party* depicts a series of figures close to the foreground plane set against a lush background of garden trees. For a prototype of the deeper landscape seen in Maillol's tapestry *Music for a Bored Princess* (fig. 26), one can recall Denis's *April* (1892), which uses an imaginary landscape setting with a road leading the eye back into space and shows a mystical procession of virgins.

The first tapestry Maillol created, entitled *Girls in a Park* (fig. 21),[32] was woven with commerical wools, probably purchased by Daniel de Monfreid.[33] Unfortunately, these chemically-dyed wools are extremely light-sensitive, and the colors eventually became bleached by exposure to sunlight.[34]

Girls in a Park depicts three women and three younger girls in a park, or garden. The figures stand in a narrow foreground plane, aligned one next to the other, engaged in no discernible activity. Here, specifically, one notes a resemblance to the fashion plate format in the frieze-like arrangement of the figures. The viewer perceives one figure after another without any strong focus. But, one should recall that Puvis de Chavanness' murals, such as the Sorbonne hemicycle, are constructed in this way, as is Seurat's *La Grande Jatte*. In this tapestry, the synthetic simplicity of these paintings is replaced by a more medieval richness of patterning.

In Maillol's paintings, as we have seen, there are never more than two figures. With the exception of *The Bather,* the number of figures in each tapestry composition ranges from four to seven. Maillol told Cladel: "I did not find my means of expression in painting, I found it in tapestry . . . It was with tapestry that I began to make compositions."[35] Maillol understood the limitations of his paintings and recognized the fact that he could create harmonious, clear compositions on a larger and more complex scale in the medium of tapestry than he could in paint. His manipulation of these groups compositionally is one of the most interesting aspects of these works. With the increased complexity of the compositions, one can observe a deeper level of ambiguity and richness of symbolism than was apparent in the earlier paintings.

Although *Girls in a Park* (fig. 21) is Maillol's earliest tapestry, all the essential iconographic elements of his later works are present: an exterior setting, women in contemporary costume, the frozen attitudes of the figures, and the division of the space into two layers, a plane on which the figures stand and a backdrop.

When *Girls in a Park* (fig. 21) was shown at the Salon de la Libre Esthétique in Brussels in 1894, Gauguin wrote in a "petit revue" in *Essais d'art libre:* "Maillol has shown a tapestry which one dare not praise too highly."[36] Perhaps Gauguin appreciated the posed, stiff, and consequently nonanecdotal quality which was also to be present in all Maillol's subsequent tapestries. None of the figures actually relate psychologically to each other. We cannot tell who is the mother of each child. From Maillol's recollection, Gauguin would have favored his avoidance of traditional methods of modeling and perspective.[37]

But it is very possible that one need not look too closely for specific elements which might have appealed to Gauguin. He might have sensed in a general way that Maillol's tapestry was on the right track. Denis has said of Maillol's works of the 1890s: "He escaped like us [the Nabis] and after us from the absurd alternative of Idealism or Naturalism, that is to say, of conventional embellishment or servile imitation.[38] Often the distinctions that can be easily drawn between works of art with our modern historical perspective were simply not relevant to the artists who were actually in the midst of a movement.

In this first tapestry, Maillol is testing different possibilities for handling drapery to see what is best suited to the medium. There is a clear distinction betweeen the flattened depiction of the central woman's dress and the curves and roundness of the seated figure's costume. Also one can see a difference in the emphasis placed on the contours of the figures. The central figure seems to be outlined distinctly against the background while the contour of the seated figure and her dress are hardly emphasized at all. These differences contribute to a general lack of unity in the work. One senses an experimental spirit where each figure is solving a certain formal problem posed by the artist.

The Enchanted Garden (fig. 22) is the second full-scale tapestry which Maillol created.[39] It presents four women in a vertical format. The two figures on the left are shown full length, from behind, while two other women stand behind them and to the right, peering through the branches of a tree. As in *Girls in a Park* (fig. 21) the composition is surrounded by a decorative plant border, similar to late medieval tapestry borders. I suggest that this work is the "Broderie" which was exhibited at the Salon de la Libre Esthétique in Brussels in 1894. It would then date from 1893-94.

Although Maillol is faithful to his theme of women in a garden, this work is more sophisticated thematically than the first tapestry. The composition is tighter and more complex and the work conveys a definite aura of mystery. The two frontal figures seem lost in conversation with one another. What then is the purpose of the two women in the rear? Are they spying or eavesdropping on the frontal pair, or are they, too, merely innocent strollers in a beautiful setting? The title of this work, referring now specifically to Blanc, expresses the otherworldly mood conveyed by this perplexing image. The tapestry manages to spin the viewer into flights of imaginary ponderings—that world of "poetry" which Blanc saw as the proper sphere of tapestry.

The women strolling through the gardens resist our attempts to discern their situation. The many possible combinations of relationships provide the viewer with an unending source of fanciful musing. The women seem to be walking through their lush setting, yet they are fixed within the borders of the tapestry, making permanent an evasive and mysterious image.

Again, the horizon line is very high, and the figures are all located close to the picture plane. There are two trees in the upper right corner, which are one-fourth the height of the tree in the foreground. Logically, these little trees should pull the viewer's eye back into space, but they do not function this way visually, since their foliage echoes the forms of the flowers in the lower left foreground and in the decorative border. The even spacing of the bright madder and indigo blue over the surface serves to further tie the different spatial planes together visually. Therefore, each element is locked into a surface pattern, in accordance with Maillol's stated intention, quoted above.

The wools used in *The Enchanted Garden* and all Maillol's subsequent tapestries are colored with plant dyes which Maillol developed himself.[40] Cladel tells us that Maillol would go into the countryside with Clotilde, his wife, armed only with "Roret's manual and a 'very curious' old book loaned by a pharmacist, one of his friends . . . "[41] He collected the plants, often finding the proper seed or berry for his dyes merely by chance, and then returned to Banyuls to prepare the solutions in which he soaked the wools. He selected pure yarn, free of any chemicals.

Naturally, the use of plant dyes severely limited the range of possible colors. For example, in *The Enchanted Garden* there is only one strong blue, no doubt, the Guatemalan indigo dye which Cladel mentions,[42] two greens, four browns, ranging from a chocolate color to a very pale beige, a deep madder red, a bright pink and gold thread. These nine colors are in marked contrast to the hundreds of chemical dyes which the Gobelins tapestry factory was using at this time. Later in his life, a chemist from the Gobelins told Maillol: "Your dyes are more beautiful than ours."[43] Maillol dryly told Cladel: "This remark of the chemist was the only encouragement I received from the Gobelins.[44]

One of Maillol's most specific adaptations from medieval tapestries lies in this limitation of colors. In the Middle Ages, all dyes were plant dyes and a relatively narrow range of colors was used. Instead of using a middle tone, Maillol alternates threads of two colors to create his halftones. This is particularly evident in the folds of the skirts of the two women in the foreground. To indicate the roundness of a tree trunk or the face of a woman, he avoids a subtle range from light to dark (again, in accordance with Blanc's instructions) and simply shifts to a darker tonality, i.e., from a light tan to a darker beige. Medieval tapestries employ a similar method for depicting halftones and Maillol's technique was probably derived from his study of those tapestries. However, the avoidance of mixed halftones was also a practice within the artistic milieu of the 1890s. Seurat had been experimenting with the possibilities of optical rather than chemical mixture of colors since the early 1880s, influenced by the writings of Delacroix, Chevreul, and Blanc. By the early 1890s, Fénéon's articles had elaborated the theory for the public. Maillol's awareness of these contemporary ideas could well have made him particularly sensitive to this aspect of medieval tapestries and encouraged him to adopt it for his own compositions.

Another aspect of *The Enchanted Garden* which surely derives from Maillol's study of medieval works of art is the richness and costliness of the materials. Gold thread has been used extensively in the yokes of the dress of the figure on the far right. The waistband and neckline of the figure next to her have been encrusted with a rich brocade. Just as the medieval craftsmen encrusted their reliquaries and icons with gold and semiprecious stones, so has Maillol created a precious object, conveyed through the preciousness of the materials themselves.

Each part of this work, the dresses, the chignons, even the parrot has been subjected to a clarification of outline and a simplification which clearly indicates that Maillol has grasped their stylistic worth. This becomes clear when one studies the drawing Maillol made for the heads of the two women on the right. Virtually all detail has been suppressed: only the contours of the profiles and the outlines of the heads are emphasized. (This is consistent with Morris's statement stressing the silhouette, in tapestry.) In this respect, one is reminded immediately of Maillol's profile paintings, particularly of the second group with foliated backgrounds in which the linear motif of the profile is much more important than interior modelling or other details. One can observe a similar simplification of the face in this tapestry; it is one flat plane set on the surface. Although this is only Maillol's second tapestry, he is beginning to show an understanding of the requirements of the medium, the need for simplified forms which can be read clearly from a distance and which do not violate the surface plane. He has also accented the decorative arabesque of the contour of the skirts, in the sweep from the waists and the smoothly curving hems, which flow with an Art Nouveau elegance.

Maillol seems to have been quite fascinated with the possibilities of the basic format of *The Enchanted Garden,* i.e., a group of four standing women in a garden. He explored this arrangement in two drawings and an oil sketch, *The Apple Pickers.*[45]

Between 1895 and 1896-97, Maillol created two tapestries which depict groups of women seated in a circle in which one figure is holding an open book and, presumably, reading aloud. *Young Women in a Park* (fig. 23), the earlier of the two, is a densely crowded work like *The Enchanted Garden* which also has too little space for the number of figures depicted. The seven women of this tapestry are almost piled on top of each other. It is impossible to imagine how all their legs and skirts could possibly fit into the space provided for them.

The Book (fig. 24), the other tapestry which depicts this motif, is only known through a woodcut.[46] In this work, only four women are depicted in a circle and the *horror vacui* of the earlier version of the motif has been replaced by a more graceful, comfortable arrangement. The composition of *Music* or *The Concert of Women* (fig. 25), Maillol's next executed tapestry, is a variant on the four-figured circle of *The Book.*

The motif of reading from a book provided Maillol with a rationale for a static gathering of women, a plausible, yet not overly specific activity. The figures are united through the shared experience of listening to the reading, yet the motif can still provide the necessary ambiguity that permits the viewer the freedom to exercise his imagination. One is provoked by the rapt attention of the listeners to wonder what is in the book? Is it a key to the secrets of life? Does it contain new perceptions of the world for these inexperienced or uninitiated maidens? What are they learning from the book? What purpose or needs does it fulfill? These questions obviously cannot be answered by the information provided in the tapestries; yet it is to Maillol's credit that his images can provoke them.

Nabi paintings, which almost never depict action or movement, are filled with activities that have been termed "silent rituals."[47] Most often these "rituals" are common activities such as dances, bathing, sewing parties. These pursuits are raised above the ordinary into the realm of a ritual by the carefully constructed, nonanecdotal way in which they are depicted. For example, Vallotton's *Bathers* and Renoir's *The Large Bathers*[48] both depict a gathering of nude women by a riverside. Renoir's image, however, is playful, lively, and although it is more posed than a typical Impressionist canvas, it possesses a sense of the momentary and the ordinary. Vallotton's figures, in contrast, are schematized; poses are frozen; faces set in expressionless masks, placed in an unnaturalistic landscape. One could cite any number of other comparisons to document this basic difference in approach between Impressionist Naturalism and Symbolism.

Maillol takes an ordinary group of women seated on a park bench listening to a reader, and with careful construction, frozen forms, and intense expressions converts the episode into a ritual. In all his tapestries, Maillol's designs seek to impart extraordinary connotations to common activities. Several of Maillol's tapestry cartoons depict anecdotal, lighthearted subjects. For example, Maillol painted two versions of *The Swing.* This is a delightful motif, very gay and charming. But it describes an action frozen in midair. It only captures a moment and implies nothing else. Another cartoon, *The Brook,* shows a woman seated in a landscape by a stream. It, too, has a momentary quality and a playful subject. Significantly, these designs lack the symbolism of the completed works, and were never actually executed as tapestries.

The specific motif of reading from a book, however, is one not encountered in the Nabi repertoire. It is possible that Maillol knew a painting by Burne-Jones, *Green Summer* (1864), which shows a similar gathering of young women seated in a landscape listening to a figure reading from a book. The group is approximately the same size as *Young Women in a Park,* and the women are seated in a similar circle. Burne-Jones's painting is quite close to Maillol's work, not only in subject matter, but also in the quiet, spiritualized, almost idyllic mood of the painting.

One should also mention as a possible source a painting by Memling, *The Mystic Marriage of St. Catherine,* in the Louvre. The Madonna and child, seated in a garden, are surrounded by six female saints, two of whom conspicuously hold open books. Actually, there are many fifteenth-century depictions of the Madonna, herself, reading in an enclosed garden. These could well be distant ancestors of Maillol's tapestries.

In *The Book* and *Young Women in a Park* one notes the typical high horizon line, which in both works is punctuated by a row of tree trunks, providing a rhythmic series of vertical accents. This pattern of tree trunks is a device seen in many Japanese woodcuts circulating in France during this period.[49] For these tapestries, Maillol has abandoned the rather volumetric drapery treatment of *The Enchanted Garden* for a flattened pattern of planes articulated with darker-toned lines.

The Book was probably the last tapestry Maillol executed in Banyuls before his departure for Paris in 1895. Having exhausted his financial resources, he could not maintain his workshop. The patronage of the Princess Bibesco, introduced to him by Vuillard a few years later, enabled him to continue his work. Princess Bibesco commissioned two large tapestries, *Music* (or *The Concert of Women*) (fig. 25) and *Music for a Bored Princess* (fig. 26).[50]

These tapestries depict three lute players and a listener, an intimate female concert, located in the ubiquitous garden setting. The quality of ritual, noted in connection with *Young Women in a Park* is very strong in these two tapestries. Like the motif of reading from a book, the concert also served Maillol's purposes well since it provided an activity which involved no action but united the group emotionally.

Maillol did not invent the motif of a concert outdoors. To understand the meaning of these two works it is necessary to trace, briefly, the history of the concert in the visual arts. Music-making has long been associated with Venus and the general activities of courtly love. Examples of concerts in medieval tapestries were actually a rather common motif and can be traced back to a fresco in Herculaneum.[51] Mirimonde, who even refers to musicians as "children of Venus," traces the recurrence of the concert motif, especially in the fifteenth and sixteenth centuries, in allegories of love.[52] For example, a sixteenth-century *millefleurs* tapestry, *La Fontaine d'amour*, in the Musée de Cluny depicts a lutist, a woman playing an organ, and a violinist. A fifteenth-century Netherlandish engraving, the *Large Garden of Love*, includes a small concert. Concerts are represented in the seventeenth century by Annibale Carracci, in a particularly charming painting by Domenichino in the Louvre, and in many of Claude Lorraine's pastoral fantasies. Watteau pursues the theme in a series of delightful works. Emile Bernard's *Medieval Scene* (1892) is a more contemporary version of the lover's concert in which a young man serenades a medieval princess while two pairs of lovers stroll through a garden.

But perhaps the most famous image of a concert, *en plein air*, is the *Concert champêtre*, attributed to Giorgione.[53] The juxtaposition of two voluptuous nudes and two fully clothed men, one of whom plays a stringed instrument is unique, and an historically accurate iconographic interpretation remains obscure, today, as in the late nineteenth century.[54] In 1913, a critic wrote that "Giorgione evokes goddesses and transports us into the unnatural world of dreams... "[55] Mirimonde felt that the work was shrouded in "an atmosphere of mystery"[56] which provoked in the viewer "a voluptuous and melancholic revery."[57] Maillol has managed to incorporate both the ambiguity and the wistful melancholy of Giorgione's painting into this tapestry.

The air of mystery in *Music* and *Music for a Bored Princess* derives in part not from the activity itself, but from the absence of men. Given the strong associations, in the history of art, between music and lovemaking, this factor is particularly striking in the context of a concert. Thus, the dreamlike quality of the work is enhanced since the figures are not actually related to one another as they would be in an allegory of love, and the relationships among the participants are left unexplained.

The tapestry conveys a sense of a quiet idyll, a world of indefinitely expanding time, to be spent in gentle pursuits. One can almost hear the delicate strumming of a ballad, transporting us away from the concerns of our daily existence. Maillol loved to listen to music, especially Mozart, after his work was done.[58] Music was his means of release from the present and the motif of the concert takes on this connotation in his works. Therefore, Maillol has managed to combine the three things he loved most—women, music and a contact with nature—into a coherent design.

It is tempting to suppose that Maillol knew that musicians were often associated in the late Middle Ages with the concept of Paradise, and musical angels were often included in Marian gardens.[59] The quality of a paradise is strongly evoked in Maillol's tapestry. Octave Mirbeau wrote a lovely passage, capturing the lyrical mood of the image:

One dare not reject this tapestry for the Salon of the Champ-de-Mars, ... The subject is simple and infinitely gracious. In a marvelously flowered garden, under trees with balanced branches, women are seated, women and not muses. ... The little peasant from the Pyrenees is already a great charmer. It is impossible to dream of an atmosphere, a more delicious decor of joy and peace, more elegant forms, more serene attitudes, a sweetness of tones of a more sparkling and harmonious brightness.[60]

In *The Concert of Women* the listener, the most important figure, is seated in the center of the composition.[61] She is rigidly positioned; her stiff back leans against a tree; she gazes out at the viewer. (Lassen likens the rigidity of the pose to the figures in Maillol's first tapestry, *Girls in a Park*.)[62] The face and features of the listener are quite similar to the crisp linearity of the *Portrait of Mme. Maillol* (fig. 10). She is thus clearly distinguished from the mandolin players whose dresses and hairdos are described in flowing, *Art Nouveau* contours. One can almost sense Maillol's attempt to provide a visual metaphor in their form for the gently flowing melody of the music. The play of line moving across the surface, linking the three musicians, is analogous to the mellifluous fluidity of a song. Just as the faces of the two side figures are averted from us, so is the precise meaning of a musical passage impossible to define in words.

It should be noted that the four figures seem to be seated in a circle which is denied, however, by the very close overlapping of the two central figures. As Howaldt has correctly noticed, the listener and the central mandolin player seem to be positioned almost one on top of the other and only the two side figures bending inwards impart the impression of a circular arrangement.[63] She attributes this to the influence of medieval tapestries, where the figures generally do not decrease in size as they move back in space. This technique maintains the integrity of the picture plane, which, as we have noted above, was one of Maillol's (and the Nabis') prime concerns.

The drapery patterns also create an effect of flatness. As opposed to the method he used in the two preceding tapestries, Maillol has chosen to emphasize the forms of the bodies beneath the skirts. He presents fairly simple, broad areas of unified color in the dresses. This emphasizes the planes of space parallel to the picture plane rather than volumes which move back and forth in space. Maillol is asserting the flatness not only of the tapestry, but also of the wall upon which it is hung. A limited range of plant dyed colors, mostly greens, golds and browns predominate; and their even distribution would further knit the foreground and background into a cohesive design.

Music for a Bored Princess (fig. 26) is the title by which Maillol, himself, identified the second tapestry commissioned by Princess Bibesco. Cladel tells us it was exhibited in a Salon and it is very possible that this tapestry was the one Maillol showed at the Salon de la Société Nationale des Beaux Arts, no. 300, in 1897.

Music for a Bored Princess is almost square. Three women, two with mandolins, sit in the upper left section of the tapestry, while the Princess sits opposite from them. A pathway divides the composition diagonally, which recalls the diagonal placement of the bench in *Young Women in a Park*. The connotations of the garden setting and the musical concert, discussed above, are relevant for this work as well. The color scheme and technical execution (regular stitches, one centimeter in height) are very similar to *Music*.

The women of *Music* were clearly identifiable as belonging to the contemporary world by their dresses, the typical 1890s leg-of-mutton sleeves and their chignon hair styles. By contrast, the figures in *Music for a Bored Princess* seem quite archaic. Maillol has reached back over the history of art to Persian miniatures and Piero della Francesca for sources for the stiffer, more primitive forms of the women in this tapestry.

The group of three women is an extremely compact mass within the composition. The distance from neck to waist seems to be drastically shortened; the proportions are very squat. The broad faces of the three women only contribute to this impression. These rounded visages, set on strong columnar necks, framed by short curly hair, clearly recall the three angels standing on the left, in the *Baptism of Christ* by Piero della Francesca.[64] The geometricized forms of the faces, which yet manage to remain those of real people, might easily have attracted Maillol. Perhaps the simplicity and the synthetic character of Piero's figures appealed to him since he was trying to incorporate these qualities into his tapestry, as well as his sculpture. It is interesting that Maillol selected figures of angels as the source for his three musicians. Piero's angels cannot by their nature belong to the real world, yet in the context of the *Baptism* they seem quite solid and tangible. This is similar to the way Maillol's tapestry images depict "real" people, yet convey the feeling of not belonging to the world we know.

The dresses of these figures are more severe than those in *Music*, without the flowing sleeves and swirling skirts of the earlier work. The skirts of the two mandolin players are solid planes of color with four areas of a lighter tone to relieve the plane. The indications of folds in the dress of the musician on the left is also very restrained; they resemble decorative stripes more than volumetric folds. The use of linear patterns to indicate a form of undulation of a surface appears in several of Gauguin's Tahitian paintings such as *Sous les Pandanus (I Raro Te Oviri)*[65] and *L'Homme à la hache*,[66] both from 1891. The conversion of rippling water into linear patterns can be traced back to Japanese woodcuts, as noted in connection with Maillol's painting *The Mediterranean* (fig. 15).

The princess has a quite different appearance from her three companions. Her features are more delicate, her head is gently inclined. Great attention has been paid to her skirt which is piled on the ground in great folds. The rigorous simplification and geometric solidity of the musician group is here replaced by a softer, vulnerable-looking creature, built of gentle curves, with the exception of the straight arm supporting her weight. In several ways, she resembles figures in Persian miniatures: her tilted head, the almost schematic treatment of the features, the intricate pattern of the shawl and the beading around her neck are all motifs which occur quite frequently in Persian miniature painting of the fourteenth to sixteenth centuries. While the appearance and spirit of the princess is quite exotic, and non-European, her pose is undoubtedly taken from a Tahitian painting by Gauguin, *Aha Oe Feii?*,[67] which was exhibited in Paris in 1893.[68]

The seated figure is also related to the figure in *Girl Tending Cows* (fig. 2), an earlier painting by Maillol. In that work, one sees the same type of young woman, seated on the ground in a traditional pose of meditation.

In *Music for a Bored Princess* Maillol has combined, in an interesting way, a wide variety of influences and has managed to maintain a unified composition in which no single element jars the synthesized impression of the whole. He has sought a different appearance for this tapestry than in his earlier works, one specifically removed from a contemporary context. In addition to the specific archaizing formal references, the use of the word "Princess" in the title also situates the scene outside of the artist's own milieu. Although the patroness of this tapestry was actually a modern princess, as a rule, princesses are special creatures, set apart from ordinary women in any age, but especially distinct from the nineteenth-century industrialized world. Merely the word "Princess" evokes images of medieval society. Perhaps Maillol's study of Persian paintings which typically depict court life suggested the use of a princess to him. Princesses appear regularly in Pre-Raphaelite paintings as well: Burne-Jones painted *The King's Daughters* (1858-59) which shows a group of young princesses picking fruit in a garden. Casting young women in the role of princesses appealed, of course, to the Pre-Raphaelite cult of the medieval. Naturally, Maillol knew many examples of young women in medieval tapestries who could easily be princesses. He had also just recently come into contact with the real Princess Bibesco.

We are also given the additional information in the title that our Princess is bored; therefore, the concert must be an amusement. One wonders why she is bored. Is she waiting for the men to return, or is she truly melancholy, pining for an unrequited love? As in all Maillol's tapestries, there are no definite answers to these questions. The image is suffused with an air of ambiguity.

Two aspects of the tapestry remain to be discussed. The three plus one composition, not seen before in Maillol's works, is a characteristic Nabi device. Sérusier, in particular, often uses a group of three women and one set apart; Maillol might well have been familiar with such images.[69]

A rather curious aspect of this tapestry is the road which winds from the lower left corner between the princess and the mandolin players upwards and back toward the upper right corner. It is clearly set in perspective and provides the viewer with a visual road to follow back into space. In his other tapestries Maillol consistently avoided such perspective devices, establishing a very shallow, flattened space. It is difficult to understand why he would tempt the delicate unity of a tapestry with an almost simplistically clear movement back into space. Perhaps it was the challenge of uniting the fundamentally flat character of a tapestry with an illusionistic, perspectively constructed space. A parallel row of tree trunks punctuates the upper background space, a motif used in several earlier tapestries, and, as noted above, one which can be traced to Japanese sources, via Bernard.

Maillol completed one other tapestry, *The Bather* (fig. 27), before the onset of his debilitating eye disease around 1900.[70] The tapestry presents the form of a seated nude woman, right hand placed across her stomach, left arm braced against a corner of brown earth. She is positioned before a solid wall of green and blue water with highlights of white foam. The upper left corner is a solid patch of beige and represents the only open space in the tapestry. The position of the figure is virtually identical to that of the Princess in *Music for a Bored Princess,* but the theme of a nude in the water relates the tapestry directly to Maillol's paintings of the same subject, especially *The Wave* (fig. 14).

The Bather is a very impressive monumental image, eliminating all but the most essential details. The tight patterning and *horror vacui* of his earlier works is now replaced with a calm and beautifully simple expression. In this last tapestry Maillol has eliminated all the medieval detail and poetic mystery of *Music for a Bored Princess* in favor of a pure, classical form. Howaldt has described this work as the most powerful decorative image ever created by a French tapestry-maker.[71]

The body is much fuller and more voluptuous than we have yet seen in these tapestries. The figure is much closer in body type to the "typical" Maillol sculpted female. Lassen attributes this development toward a fullness of form to the influence of Renoir's paintings. The slender, stiff women of *Music for a Bored Princess* and even the slender clothed figures of *Young Women in a Park* have yielded here to what Lassen feels is a more sculpturesque, plastic conception of the female form. He believes that Renoir's influence was a vital factor in freeing Maillol from the flat, decorative style of the Gauguin circle.[72] It has been mentioned in connection with the paintings that Maillol was familiar with Renoir's oeuvre. Whether one can attribute the appearance of this image exclusively to the influence of Renoir is debatable.

The movement toward a greater simplification and monumentalization of form and consequently a strong, unified visual impact was visible in Maillol's painted works from 1895-96: *The Mediterranean* (fig. 15), *The Wave* (fig. 14) and *The Woman and the Wave* (fig. 16). The connections between this tapestry and the last painting are particularly close since the drapery crosses her body in the same way. That painting dates from 1896. There would only be a small time lag between the painting and the execution of this tapestry.[73] We have seen that the group of paintings to which *The Woman and the Wave* belongs was based originally upon an image by Gauguin, *Ondine.*

Parallelling a similar development in his painting and sculpture, Maillol has moved away from the small, intimate patterns of late-medieval tapestries and aligned himself fully with the synthetic forms of Gauguin's nudes, especially from the Tahitian period.[74] In addition to the connection with Gauguin's *Ondine,* the motif of the straight arm with the hand bent inwards at a right angle is one Gauguin used repeatedly. Maillol has borrowed not only that specific motif but the undetailed smoothly curving quality of Gauguin's large nudes in *Et l'Or de leur corps* (W. 596) and *Aha Oe Feii?* (W. 461), for example. Therefore, this stylistic change is not necessarily a rejection of Gauguin's influence in favor of Renoir's as Lassen maintains.

The Bather clearly anticipates Maillol's sculptural production.[75] The broad planes and smoothly rounded contours are the strongest stylistic elements of the first large-scale statue, *The Mediterranean* (1900-05).[76] The tapestry, therefore, provides a link between an image designed for a flat surface and Maillol's mature style of large sculpture. It is not the only work which can be viewed in this context, but it is the only surviving tapestry which embodies a clearly synthetic, classically simplified treatment of the nude female form, a form which Maillol will use consistently only after 1900.

Cladel tells us that, with the financial backing of the Bibesco family and others, Maillol finally had enough money to purchase a loom to make true, woven tapestries. He set to work, and the tapestry was one-third finished when his eyesight weakened and he was forced to abandon it. He had been working by lamplight as well as during the days, and the strain on his eyes was too great.[77] The only evidence which has survived of this last unfinished work are two cartoons (fig. 28).[78] They are both of the same subject: two women seated next to one another in a landscape of indeterminate nature.

The positioning of these figures shows a desire to create a geometrical abstraction of their bodies. In the figure on the left, the woman's right arm juts out at a right angle to her body. Her other arm is completely extended straight down by her side. Her head is turned sharply away from the other figure, in a strict profile. The body of the woman on the left has also been bent in a sharp angle. The line of her upper leg is perfectly parallel to the groundline. The negative space defined by arm, torso, and leg is an equilateral triangle. Her head seems tilted at exactly a forty-five-degree angle. The limbs of these women seem to have been spread in an almost pinwheel manner, flattening their forms drastically.

While we have not seen this angularity in Maillol's painted oeuvre the figures are similar to several of Maillol's sculpted reliefs, especially *Desire*

(1906-8) (Gug. 51)[79] However, it is still a rather unexpected stylistic evolution for the artist, one that is impossible to analyze, as it was cut off so sharply. This last tapestry design does indicate Maillol's growing security in manipulating the form of the female body to achieve a given aesthetic impact—a development which will only be expressed in sculpture. *Desire* is a remarkable formal arrangement of two complete figures within a square frame.

The abstract, geometric control Maillol brought to this relief was not lost on the next generation of artists. Raymond Duchamp-Villon carried Maillol's image to its logical conclusion in his *Lovers* (1913) where the limbs of the figures become simplified tubular protuberances from the support.

When one attempts to summarize Maillol's development as a tapestry-maker, the fertility of his imagination is one of the most impressive elements. Each major work represents a change of some sort, and it is clear that Maillol viewed each new tapestry as a creative challenge. During the years of his activity, his conceptions were constantly evolving.

In the progression of tapestry compositions from *The Enchanted Garden,* through the two tapestries with the book motif, to *The Concert of Women* and *Music for a Bored Princess,* one sees a progression toward a greater clarity of organization of the figures. Maillol moved from a composition which squeezes as many figures as possible into an inadequate space toward an organization of figures into clear groups *(Music for a Bored Princess)* or spaced out evenly across the tapestry surface *(Music).* The advantages of the latter arrangement are obvious. From a cramped, overly patterned composition which is difficult to decipher, one moves into a harmonious arrangement of figures. Clearly, with each new tapestry, Maillol was seeking to improve upon the compositional solutions of his last work.

Furthermore, each tapestry reveals a different treatment of drapery folds as well as individual dress designs. Maillol never developed a set of formulae for any of the elements in his tapestries; the vegetation, or the figures, and the drapery is no exception to this rule.

However, the formal achievements in a fairly intractable medium should not overshadow the fact that his compositions are quite complex, ambiguous and intriguing. It is to Maillol's credit that he could manipulate fairly ordinary images (there are no cult symbols, no ritualistic trappings) to create in each tapestry a situation where one knows that things are not simply what they seem, yet one cannot say what exactly is happening. One senses strongly a significance for the groupings; these women are not gathered together by chance. Yet, ultimately, one is left unsure of so many things. The viewer is constantly guessing, which is precisely what Maillol wanted.

Taken as a group, the tapestries are remarkably beautiful and quite original creations. Maillol managed in this medium to achieve the goal which eluded him in his paintings. Perhaps this is why he summed up his experiences by saying: "The epoch of the tapestries was the happiest of my life."[80]

4

Sculpture of the 1890s

Cladel describes the beginning of Maillol's activities in sculpture:

> In the studio at Banyuls, while standing near the loom, supervising the activity of his workers and selecting the tones of the wool, his hands, his diligent hands, animated with a constant need for creation, worked, one could say, by themselves. Remembering his modeling exercises at the Ecole des Arts Décoratifs . . . [1] he took up the rustic pocket knife of the artist-artisan and began to carve pieces of wood; walnut, pear or olive. [2]

Later, in Cladel's biography, Maillol discusses his feelings about sculpting directly in the block: "The sculptor takes a block and obtains from it at first a head or a figure, based on a rough sketch which suffices as a guide. This is the way I started when carving wooden statuettes."[3] "Without hesitation, Maillol launched himself quite naturally into *direct carving* . . . "[4] There is no external evidence to contradict this version of Maillol's sculptural début.

Around 1894-95, while Maillol supervised his tapestry workers, he turned to wood carving almost as an amusement or pastime. Among his very first pieces of sculpture are a series of bas-reliefs (both carved in wood and modeled in clay). One should remember that Maillol began his career as a sculptor with all the training, visual patterns and conceptions of a painter. Not only do his first statues reflect this predisposition but also his later works will bear this imprint. Therefore, it is not surprising that for these reliefs Maillol adapted images which he had previously developed for a painting or tapestry, rather than designing compositions specifically for the new medium. Maillol had, as noted above, freely transposed an image conceived for a painting or tapestry into another two-dimensional medium, such as a woodcut or a lithograph. In this early phase, he simply transfers a flat design into a fairly shallow relief. He will maintain the principle of a single viewpoint that is inherent in a painting in his early statuettes as well.

Two of these very early reliefs are carved in circular sections of fruitwood, varnished to a dark brown. *Figure with a Mandolin*[5] recreates the central mandolin player from the tapestry *Music* (fig. 25). The position of the figure is identical to the tapestry image. The dress style is the same, but the deep folds of cloth in the sleeves and shirt have been emphasized in the relief. A tree, positioned on the right, bends about the figure's head, providing the symbol of a natural setting which, as we have seen, was also included in all his paintings.

The second wooden bas-relief, *Figure in a Meditative Pose* (fig. 29), depicts a clothed female figure seated on the ground in a traditional contemplative pose. Her gaze is directed downwards and her head is supported on her hand. This motif is one of Maillol's favorites, which he developed over a fifteen-year period.[6]

It appears that Maillol did not feel strongly that sculpture necessarily meant either carving into the block or modeling. At roughly the same time he began to carve his statuettes and reliefs, he began modeling in clay; statuettes, reliefs and pottery. He continued to practice both carving and modeling throughout his career. Sometime during his extended stay in Banyuls, between 1893 and 1895, he discovered a clay bed on the outskirts of the town from which he extracted clay. His interest in the art of ceramics only increased during the following years. Maillol must have derived a certain amount of satisfaction from this activity since he persisted in this medium despite the difficulties in properly firing his works. (In 1897, he was baking his pottery in Monfreid's oven.)[7] At Banyuls, "he built a kiln himself, and without scientific information, depending as always on his instinct, he baked by chance, accepting philosophically the first disappointments, clay cracked, burst into pieces, reduced to powder...."[8]

Maillol painted *The Wave* (fig. 14) in 1895; shortly thereafter, he was sufficiently satisfied with his image to reproduce it almost exactly in a terracotta bas-relief.[9] The figures are virtually identical except the straight line of the back of the painted figure has been curved from the shoulder blade to accommodate the circular format of the relief. The figure is modeled in an extremely low relief. The waves are, physically, less than one centimeter deep. Surely such a work is as close to a two-dimensional rendition as is possible in clay and parallels, in this respect, Maillol's wooden reliefs.

The other reliefs from this period are among Maillol's earliest pieces of sculpture: an ornamental frame for a mirror (fig. 30) and a headboard for a crib (fig. 31), made for his son Lucien, who was born in 1896.[10] The mirror is crowned by a relief of *Leda and the Swan*, a subject to which Maillol returned around 1902. Again, he has adapted an image created in paint for his figure. Leda's position is very close to that of *Bather Seated on a White Drapery* (fig. 13) and recalls those sources mentioned in connection with that painting— Renoir's *Large Bathers* and Michelangelo's *Night*. The frame itself is divided into an interior and an exterior border. The design of the exterior rim consists of an abstract geometric zig-zag pattern.

The headboard of the crib shows "two angels inspired by the Italian Renaissance"[11] in profile, kneeling facing one another with hands raised in a gesture of prayer. This type of kneeling angel is seen in many Quattrocento paintings and was especially popular in Lombard sculpture. A similar angel, the Angel of the Annunciation, can be seen in Tullio Lombardo's *Vendramin Monument,* for example.[12] Maillol's basic instincts of design remain consistent: he applies the same kinds of influences to his three-dimensional works as he does to his paintings. The crib was carved within a year of the *Portrait of Mme. Maillol,* which also has a strong Quattrocento flavor. The designs of both the crib and the mirror are strictly symmetrical.

While these carved reliefs provide us with one connection between Maillol's two-dimensional and three-dimensional works, three large ceramic fountains provide another. These fountains are a combination of ceramic work, drawing in glazes and relief sculpture. Each fountain consists of two separate parts: a rounded oval shaped container with a removable lid and a basin. The handle of each lid is a crouching female pouring liquid from a jug in obvious reference to the function of the fountain (figs. 32 and 33).

Fountains of this type were fairly common in eighteenth-century French ceramic production.[13] It is possible that Maillol could have purchased them ready-made and then applied his decorations in clay and glazes and refired the entire piece.[14] However, considering the availability of free clay, as well as Maillol's aversion to commercial materials, I believe that he did mold the forms himself, basing his design on an eighteenth-century type. Fountains I and II are fairly close to the traditional style for wall fountains, while the slender, elongated form of Fountain III is a more personal variation.[15] There is a clear progression from the simplest and virtually unadorned fountain, which is probably the earliest, to the larger and more complexly decorated work of the third fountain.

These fountains are most interesting when placed in the context of Maillol's development from painter and tapestry-maker to sculptor, since they bridge the various media. In Fountains II and III, Maillol decorated the surfaces with drawings in glazes. Thus he had to adapt two-dimensional drawings to the surface of a three-dimensional object. In Fountain III he used both two-dimensional drawings and figures in relief for the decoration of the body of the fountain. These works were probably created in the order in which I have numbered them, in the kiln which Vollard built for Maillol at his home in Villeneuve-St. Georges. Since they were all shown at his one-man show in 1902, they must have been created between 1897-98 and 1902.

The container of Fountain II is covered with designs in a dark blue glaze (fig. 32). The Three Graces appear on the relatively flat frontal surface in a rear, a three-quarter, and frontal view.[16] These figures are drawn with a sharp linear outline of dark blue. The shading is indicated by hatching strokes with dark blue; light blue is used as a middle tone.[17] There are also two more figures on the lateral sides of the container, separated from the three central figures by two elaborate columns of vegetal forms. The one on the right has the same pose with the sharply turned head of Maillol's statue, *Eve* (Gug. 24, 1899).

The bottom half of the container of Fountain III is decorated with a figure seen from the back and in relief (fig. 33). She appears to be seated on a small rise of land, indicated by drawn details in blue. This is the first combination of relief sculpture and drawing in the same composition.

The drawing on the rear plaque between the container and basin shows two bathers, one submerged up to her ankles in water, the other seated on the ground, holding onto a tree. The theme and treatment of this design resembles a zincograph[18] of two bathers, mentioned in relation to *The Mediterranean* (fig. 15). Thus, the series both recalls previously developed two-dimensional images and anticipates future works of sculpture. Technically as well, Maillol here manages to combine relief sculpture and drawing on a three-dimensional object in an innovative and sophisticated manner.

To my knowledge, no other contemporary artist was making ceramics on this scale. They are very carefully crafted objects which obviously occupied a large portion of his energies during his transition from painter and tapestry-maker to full-time sculptor. Mirbeau was very impressed by the third fountain. In his article of 1905, he describes this piece in detail, concluding: "[this is] an object worthy of occupying the best place in the most precious case of a museum."[19]

To some extent the group of reliefs and ceramics analyzed above are but the necessary prelude to the series of beautiful statuettes which Maillol created between 1896 and 1900. Maillol's fully three-dimensional sculpture is intimately related to his paintings and tapestries on several levels. Although superficially there appears to be a sharp break in Maillol's career, we are in fact dealing in many ways with a continually evolving oeuvre which at a certain point embraces another medium, rather than a fundamental shift of artistic concepts. Before beginning an analysis of the works themselves, it would be useful to situate the sculpture as a group within the context of Maillol's previous creations.

The most obvious link between the paintings, the tapestries, and the sculpture is the subject of women. With only one exception, Maillol's sculptural production treats the form of the female body to the exclusion of all other objects in nature. The most obvious difference between these portions of his oeuvre is the predominant nudity of the sculpture, while, in general, Maillol's two-dimensional women remain chastely dressed.[20] There are several possible reasons why Maillol avoided the nude in his early works. He might well have been reacting against the erotic nudity of Cabanel and most academic art. Denis ever refers to typical academic nudes as "pornographic photographs."[21] However, the evidence of the works points to a more practical, rather than ideological explanation. The beginnings of Maillol's efforts in sculpture occur at about the same time as the appearance of nudes in his paintings and tapestries, i.e., around 1895. In that year he was married and Mme. Maillol was available as a model; her face and body then appear constantly in Maillol's works. Since we know, from Cladel, that Maillol encountered serious difficulties finding models in Banyuls, it would seem that his marriage is the most logical explanation for the increased appearance of nude figures in his creations in all media.

In addition to the subject of women, a further factor which unites Maillol's works is an absence of action. With few exceptions Maillol's sculptured figures are posed in static positions which do not imply any movement. The women do not walk or run; their bodies do not twist in space. They sit on the ground or on an unobtrusive support, or they stand with legs together. Occasionally, they recline, but always the forms are self-contained. The gestures are very simple. Usually the arms remain close to the torso. When they are extended away from the body, they are usually not fully extended. Their positions do not involve, to any great extent, the space which the viewer occupies. As we have seen, the same principle of inactivity is apparent in Maillol's paintings and tapestries.

This conscious avoidance of the depiction of activity relates Maillol's work quite clearly to the Postimpressionist reaction to Impressionism in the 1880s and 1890s. Seurat and Gauguin were among the first artists to pursue immobility as a consciously desired quality in painting. The Turkish treatise of Sunbal-Záde-Vehbi, passed between these two in 1885-86, "enjoined the artist to give his figures static poses."[22] The artist's task, according to Nabi-Synthetist theories, was not to attempt the depiction of the transitory and fluctuating aspects of nature, as the misguided Impressionists had done, but to paint what was stable and permanent in nature. Alternately, the artist was expected to fix the images from his imagination on canvas. In either case, movement was shunned as a perversion of the true goals of the artist. Thus, this idea had become part of the avant-garde milieu in Paris well before the publication in 1893 of Hildebrandt's theoretical essay *On the Problem of Form in Painting and Sculpture,* which instructed the artist to avoid the depiction of movement in the interests of "total visual form."

Because Maillol's painted women are often depicted in bust length, gesture plays a relatively insignificant part. However, in one of Maillol's few full-length images, *Woman with an Umbrella* the figure raises a hand to her hat and in *Profile* (Gug. 114) to her head, an action very similar in nature to the gesture of *The Bather with Raised Arms* (Gug. 87, 88, 1930).[23] Each pose shows the arm raised but turning back upon the body. Just as Maillol's sculptures do not reach out into space, the equivalent containment occurs in the paintings where the women, as well as not making any gestures toward the viewer, generally do not make eye contact with the viewer. Virtually all Maillol's two-dimensional women have their eyes downcast or closed, and are usually positioned in profile, which further isolates them. One never feels as if one can penetrate, psychologically, Maillol's two-dimensional images, just as one cannot become emotionally involved in one of his sculptured women. Both types of figures are objects for contemplation, and do not elicit our direct emotional involvement, even though they do radiate thought and feelings nonspecifically. André Gide described *The Mediterranean:* "She is beautiful; she means nothing. This is a silent work."[24] He was struck by this closed-in uncommunicative character of the piece. This work does not inform the viewer of its meaning. The aura of silence which is characteristic of all Maillol's sculpture is constantly present in the paintings and tapestries as well, where the figures seem to be sunk in a deep spell.

It is now necessary to examine more specifically the form which Maillol's sculpture took, during this period. A pivotal work for his development as a sculptor is *La Source,* or *The Spring,* a wooden relief (1896) (fig. 34). Unlike the previously mentioned reliefs, it is not an adaptation of an essentially two-dimensional image and points more directly in the direction of his mature sculpture. Cladel describes the exectuion of *La Source* in some detail:

> At Banyuls, where customs remained strict, he could not dream of asking one of the young women of his circle to pose before him.... It was thus from memory that he sculpted in a piece of pear wood, a small relief, thirty-five centimeters tall. Nevertheless, one of his workers, his future sister-in-law, consented to let him see her leg. He gave the name *The Spring* to this female nude which detaches itself from the long folds of drapery, the ingenious arrangement of which makes one think of fluid sheets of water spouting cascades from the fissures of the mountain.[25]

One can easily believe that *The Spring* was not carved from life. The figure is positioned in profile, in an unnatural stance: her torso leans forward at a forty-five degree angle. The right leg, from the hip to the knees is bent in the opposite direction at an equally sharp angle, while the lower leg slants backwards again from left to right. The figure is positioned in a perfect zig-zag. A tree stands on the right, the obligatory bit of landscape that relates the work to Maillol's paintings which most often have a tree placed in just that position in the compositon. Her left hand grasps a knot of cloth to her waist. [This motif occurs in one of Maillol's paintings, *The Woman and the Wave* (fig. 16), and is repeated in the tapestry *The Bather* (fig. 27).]

The most original aspect of the relief is the proportions of the figure. She has the thickened and shortened arms and legs of Maillol's Catalan type, the proportions which he was to adapt for so many of his large-scaled figures: *Pomone, Vénus, Summer.* By Maillol's own testimony this form is inspired by the native women of Banyuls:

> "I looked at the women of my country. They busied themselves with domestic work, cooking, washing the floor, coming and going half-nude. I lifted their skirts and found marble."[26]

Maillol's comment is, of course, partly facetious. His women are not copies of any single Catalan, but a distillation, a creative interpretation based on the physical type of women he knew so well.

While *The Spring* reveals one canon of proportions, which Maillol will utilize in his later work, the *Standing Bather* (fig. 35) reveals an alternative form for the human body which will also resurface in his large-scale sculpture. Both these works stand at the very beginning of Maillol's career as a sculptor and cannot be very far apart in date. In *The Spring* the limbs, especially the ankles, thighs and upper arms, are very thick. The woman is a fairly heavy, stocky type. This is the "ben plantada" of which Cassou speaks.[27] By contrast, in the *Standing Bather,* we see an overly slender, almost tubular form. The body conforms to the narrow verticality of a tree trunk or branch: the legs are pressed together, one arm clings flatly to the length of the body, while the other is wrapped around the back. Her breasts are positioned high on the torso, hips curve very slightly outward from the waist. The torso is short; the legs long. Throughout his creative life, Maillol continued to use both anatomical types, choosing one or the other according to his expressive intents. It should be emphasized that these basic types are artificial constructions. In each sculpture, the female body is designed for a given aesthetic intent. In the case of *The Spring* and the other sculptures of this type, the ankles and wrists are thickened to impart the impression of a column to the limbs. Feet are enlarged to provide a firm base for the body. These are only the most obvious distortions of naturalistic anatomy. Each piece represents an original solution to the given problem of creating a statue which expresses certain abstract concepts, yet retains its naturalistic connections.

In the *Standing Bather* (fig. 35), one can observe an abstract control by the sculptor over the human form. The breasts and head are perfectly round, symmetrical spheres. This is a primitive's conception of the human body, in which the artist's mental image controls the form. There is virtually no naturalistic detail. Just an utterly simple rendition of the elements of the female body described with an emphasis on a geometric underpinning. In these respects, Maillol's statues recall the Egyptian and archaic Greek sculpture which the artist preferred to sculpture from later classical periods.[28] It was in reference to this figure, or one very similar to it, that Maillol recounted the following anecdote:[29]

> He saw, one day, while leafing through *La Forme,* a photo of his first statuette, held by Bernheim. He did not recognize it, and took it for a Chinese statuette. "This is sculpture, he exclaimed, you have done nothing as good as that." A name was inscribed beneath the figure which arrested him . . . he looked! It was his. "This is my first statuette. . . . What a discovery! And thus I recognized that my first work, sculpted in wood, just like that, without my knowing too much or where I was going, was a striking work."[30]

The abstract, nonnaturalistic, virtually symbolic form of the figure was recognized immediately and with great pleasure by Maillol.

This interest in geometry would be a controlling factor for the later sculpture as well. Maillol has said: "I build my figures according to a geometric plan, but I choose this plan myself. *The Mediterranean* is enclosed in a perfect square. *L'Île de France* is inscribed in a right triangle..."[31]

The *Standing Bather* (fig. 35) possesses several other characteristics which, in addition to those mentioned above, typify every one of Maillol's later pieces of sculpture: the urge to retain the limbs close to the trunk of the body, asserting the "monolithic" structure of the work of art, and the utter simplicity and nonanecdotal character of the image.[32] These qualities of form could also be applied to Maillol's paintings and tapestries. Specifically with the tapestries, the sculpture shares a sense of craftsmanship, a hand-made quality which was most important to Maillol.

These early statuettes are meant to be viewed from no more than two points in space, a frontal view and a profile one, which relates them to the characteristic poses in Maillol's paintings. In the case of the *Standing Bather* (fig. 35), the frontality of the body is only relieved by a quarter turn of the head; all essential details can be comprehended from a single vantage point in front of the statue.

In addition to these formal characteristics, the technique used to carve the sculpture relates to Maillol's experience as a painter. Maillol approached these first carved wooden statues in a strictly two-dimensional way:

> The idea came to me to carve a statue in a wood log. I marked in pencil a circle for the head, another for each shoulder, two for the breasts, one for the stomach. I worked on this canvas.... The inspiration was in me: I would become a sculptor.[33]

The *Standing Bather* is a typical example of Maillol's sculpture in wood. However, during this early phase of his career, Maillol was also modeling three-dimensional figures in clay. A group of bronze statuettes, e.g. *Clothed Nabis* (Gug. 19) and *Small Seated Woman with Chignon* (Gug. 56) represent his vision, at a very early stage of his career, as a sculptor. Vollard funded a series of bronze editions of these tiny statuettes (some are only six inches tall) around 1900, but it is likely that the original terracottas were made around 1896.[34]

These statuettes have a number of stylistic features in common: they are clothed and reveal an interest in drapery treatment. They have very slender limbs and thin hips, and their heads, which have chignons, are quite short in proportion to their total body length. What is particularly interesting in terms of Maillol's development as a sculptor is the lack of corporeality or three-dimensionality of these pieces. The breasts barely protrude, the folds of drapery appear as linear accents rather than volumetric curves. The limbs, when they are visible are so slender that the viewer's sense of tactility, or physical presence is not invoked.

The development of Maillol's typical female form in the years between 1895-96 and 1902 becomes clear when one compares the *Study for The Mediterranean* (Gug. 47) or the *Leda* (Gug. 40), both from 1900-1902, with the works discussed above. The bodies in these later pieces have filled out considerably; well-proportioned arms and legs in graceful positions have replaced the awkward attenuated limbs of the early seated pieces. Maillol does not discard his more slender type, but the heavier canon begins to play a more important role in his oeuvre. He is now exploring the fuller body forms of *The Spring* (fig. 34). This shifted emphasis parallels the change in his paintings, but occurs two or three years later. In paintings such as *Woman with an Umbrella* (fig. 4) and *Spring* (fig. 7) Maillol's women are elegant, attenuated creatures. In the group of paintings based upon the nude form of Mme. Maillol, *The Wave* (fig. 14) and *The Mediterranean* (fig. 15), the female body is built of more fully rounded, voluptuous forms.

The fullness of form in the later works reveals Maillol's increasing security in the manipulation of volumes. He has now acquired a proficiency in the handling of forms in space and can explore the female body, not as outlines and linear drapery patterns as in the earlier group, but much more as volumes of the female body. This increased fullness gives these pieces of sculpture a sense of corporeality, a real presence: their weight is more apparent and they assert themselves more forcefully as sculptural entities. The increased tangibility also conveys a strong sensuality.

Maillol was quite conscious of the importance of volumes in sculpture. In 1905, he described his conception about this particular aspect of his work in the following way:

> To model a vase, a simple pot, a humble pitcher, a bottle... or to model a breast, a torso, a young stomach, a woman's round thigh... it is but the same thing... and do you doubt it?... What is a vase? It is that, all that... it is the breast, the torso, the stomach, the thigh, the hip, the rump... it is the beautiful fruit... it is the bulb with its sexual mystery.... By modeling a vase... I apprehend and understand the human form which repeats itself to infinity, in the flowers, in the mountain, in the sky as much as in modeling the figure..., for the human form preceded the appearance on the earth of man, who has only, in order to give an appearance of equilibrium, of harmony, of beauty, to copy faithfully the forms living, swarming around him in the primitive splendors of nature.[35]

Maillol is here describing the unity he perceives in the forms of nature and their relationship to his sculpture. Certainly, if one takes him literally, the statement makes no sense: a breast is not the same form as a vase. But in the two different forms Maillol perceives a basic similarity; the quality of roundness or fullness which in a synthetic or generalized way links the two. When he strips away the superficial distinguishing details, Maillol sees the basic elements of the human body, and especially the female body, reflected in the forms of inanimate nature, and comprehended in terms of volumes.

This statement contains one of the keys to understanding Maillol's sculpture. He is saying that the basic volumes of the human form can be perceived in many aspects of inanimate nature, such as mountains and bays. Through his art, he tries to penetrate beneath the external dissimilarities to reveal the unities linking humanity and the world.[36]

It would be virtually impossible for an artist in 1890 who wished to express this concept, totally dependent on volumetric rotundities, to do so through the medium of painting; it belongs completely to the world of sculpture. In order to indicate volumes in painting, an artist must employ modeling and consequently violate the flatness of the picture plane. This was precisely what the generation of painters of the 1890s believed to epitomize all that was most misguided in their predecessor's work.

In these respects, therefore, Maillol's sculpture explores specifically sculptural properties (just as his tapestries sought to penetrate the true nature of the medium). The typical Maillol statue, whether six inches or six feet tall, possesses a tangibility which imparts a sense of actuality, one step closer to the world of real objects than any two-dimensinal work, and which forces its attention on the viewer.

In other ways, however, Maillol's sculpture reveals the artist's origins as a painter and exploits certain qualities which are usually considered to belong more properly to the sphere of painting. A two-dimensional work of art, by its nature, has only one main point of view: Maillol has carried this principle of a limited viewpoint over into his statues. With few exceptions, a Maillol sculpture is meant to be seen from only a few places, usually one directly in front of the piece, and another from the side. Moving around the sculpture not only provides no additional visual information, but also destroys the static, contemplative mood in the viewer which Maillol was trying to stimulate:

> I have only a few principal profiles and still I find there are too many of them. I would prefer to have only two profiles like the antique primitives [He then cites the pedimental sculpture at Olympia, as an example.] Their art is for me the most beautiful.[37]

This conscious avoidance of true three-dimensional sculpture which turns and moves in space or encourages the viewer to move about it may be seen as a consequence of Maillol's vision as a painter. Even the use of the term "profile" connotes a flat image. Pedimental sculpture is the closest equivalent to painting, of sculpture in the round, in the sense of the limited points in space from which it can be perceived, and the way in which the sculpture is locked into a frame. Furthermore, the sculpture of the pediments at Olympia, which Maillol says is the "most beautiful," has two clearly defined planes, the layer in which the sculpture exists and the flat surface which closes off the space behind them. This is precisely the way Maillol chose to construct so many of his paintings, where one has a figure set before a flattened landscape backdrop.

As noted above, in many paintings and the best of his tapestries, Maillol defines human forms by smoothly moving, clear contours. (The contours are not emphasized to the same extent as in *cloisonisme.)* Irregularities are eliminated, as is most internal modeling. Similarly, this well-defined graceful contour is the trademark of a Maillol statue. It is always present, and, as noted above, the "profile" of his sculpture was one of his major concerns. Mirbeau confirmed the importance of the contour in Maillol's work in the following statement:

> Among the necessary gaucheries and the charming ignorances one discerns, very clearly, his taste for beautiful lines, for logical and simple arrangements, a taste, in short, which characterizes the least of his works—statuette, pot, engraving, work in wicker, embroidered fabric, tapestry—by an accent, so moving, so different always."[38]

For one modern critic, this aspect of Maillol's sculpture was also its most significant aesthetic quality:

> The key to the artistic success of individual figures lies in the beauty of their outlines, in the elegance of their bounding arabesques. . . . Once seen properly the essential aesthetic tension between flat outline and material substance raises a Maillol nude from the prosaic to the poetic.[39]

The importance of the contour for Maillol's sculpture can be easily seen if one examines any Maillol drawing (e.g. Gug. 113, 123 and 135). A typical one consists of a heavy, dark line which defines the exterior boundary of the figure, separating it from the surrounding page, and much more gentle markings for modeling and internal details. The artist has usually traced the exterior contour line several times. This interest in the contour can be seen in the drawings from the 1890s, for example, in a preparatory drawing for *The Wave* (Gug. 116). The only indications on the page define the exterior outline. Another preparatory drawing for the heads of the two women in the foreground of the tapestry *The Enchanted Garden* shows a similar concern.

To understand the importance of the drawings as proof of Maillol's concern for the contour, one must be aware of the indispensable role drawing played in his creative process. A pair of drawings for a very early statuette, *The Washerwoman* (Gug. 21, 1896),[40] documents his dependence on drawings to help him evolve his work. Although in its final form, she is an elegant figure, with all the qualities associated with Art Nouveau—the moving arabesque of the skirt, intense interest in the details of costume and the curving lines of the arms—the subject was surely originally inspired by Maillol's observation of the women of Banyuls. In one of his statements, quoted above, Maillol mentions washing the floor as a very typical activity for the women and one which he often watched in order to study his subjects. [He also painted a version of this theme, *The Washerwomen* (fig. 18).]

A life study documents this aspect of naturalistic observation. One sees a fairly straightforward depiction of a kneeling woman; the torso is parallel to the ground, the arms fall almost vertically beneath her shoulders, while her hands cross in front of her. She gives the impression of applying pressure to the floor.[41]

The desire to stretch out the form of the figure is illustrated in another drawing.[42] Here, Maillol has created an impossible anatomical position, raising one leg and one arm completely off the ground and throwing the torso sharply downward. He is trying to expand his compact figure of the early drawing into a more flowing and elegant form.

This desire has been realized admirably in the final statuette which synthesizes the two images of the drawings. From the center of balance, located at the waist, one's eye moves forward along the line of the arm and backward, following the folds of the skirt. The detail is magnificently worked; the skirt falls from delicate pleats at the waist; the billowing leg-of-mutton sleeves have deep folds; the space between the arms is closed by a sweeping ribbon of bronze.

With these works, the picture of Maillol in the 1890s is complete. We have analyzed his personal style in painting, tapestry, and now sculpture up to 1900. This provides us not only with an understanding of an early phase of a long career, but also with a fundamental grasp on all Maillol's subsequent works, in particular, his large-scale sculpture. By 1900 and certainly by 1905, Maillol had fully developed his artistic identity. The works which he produced during the remainder of his life are, to a great extent, variations on the formulas he developed in this decade:

> Maillol's sculptured work is not divisible into periods and styles. . . . By 1900 he was a fully developed sculptor. His work was to be a series of variations on a few themes and it is this unity which gives his art its profundity and which guides his hand. . . . The *Standing Bather* [fig. 36] of 1900 carries the seed of nearly all his later work. . . . He evolves within a closed circuit.[43]

We have demonstrated the numerous interrelationships among the works in each medium, and traced the continuity of Maillol's personal style which transcends the differences in material. The remarkable unity of artistic intent extends to the large-scale sculpture and will be explored in the epilogue.

Conclusion

Looking back over Maillol's artistic production of the 1890s, one is immediately struck by the underlying unity within its great diversity. The subject of the female form is a constant in his works in all media; painting, tapestries, and sculpture. In each work, Maillol was not illustrating the specific appearance of individual women but, rather, a synthetic image of Woman. His works are not portraits, but idealized, generalized, and simplified figures. Given this formal problem, he avoided the dangers of stagnation, and created a continuously innovative body of works.

Consistent with this goal, Maillol's iconography reveals a constant reluctance to explain the full story behind his images. The viewer is required to interpret the information provided to complete the image. This reluctance to program the meaning of his works clearly separates Maillol from academic paintings and sculpture and the works of many of his contemporaries, and foreshadows the concerns of much of twentieth-century art. The consequent "mystery" is thought-provoking and stimulates the viewer to meditate on the meaning contained in these often uncommunicative images.

While, for the purposes of clarity, in this study Maillol's output was divided by media, the numerous connections between all aspects of his works, at each phase of this decade, have been analyzed in some depth in the preceding chapters. His principles of design certainly evolve over the course of this period, but, as might be expected, the contemporary works in each medium have much in common with one another.[1]

His paintings demonstrate the desire to merge women and nature into a unified image—a goal he would also pursue in his tapestries and sculpture. His most characteristic paintings show a profile image and reveal an artist attuned to the concerns and theories of the *avant-garde,* Symbolist painters of his time, trying to create original, expressive paintings. Only, after 1895 did he paint the nude figure. This is surprising, considering his future development, but not unusual within the context of contemporary Nabi paintings.

In the medium of tapestry, he created a series of very beautiful, quite unusual works, which although small in number, are very impressive creations.

His tapestries are peopled with groups of women in paradisial gardens, engaged in quiet activities which imply a secret significance which the viewer must penetrate. Unlike most of his paintings, which are not among the most important paintings of the 1890s, the tapestries are the most complex and sensitive creations in that medium from the period.

While the very early reliefs and statuettes can be viewed as a direct outgrowth of Maillol's paintings and tapestries, he quickly discarded some of these painter's concepts (while retaining others) and began to explore the problems of mass and volume which belong so specifically to sculpture. By 1900, Maillol was a fully mature sculptor and the basic vocabulary and forms of his future works of sculpture are well established. (The connection between the large sculpture and his earlier works will be explored in the Epilogue.)

Maillol's stylistic development reminds us again of the importance of the 1890s for the course of twentieth-century art. His paintings, tapestries, and the early sculpture are quite typical of Symbolist art of the period. It is easy to see their roots in the contemporary milieu. By 1900, many of the statuettes look forward to the organic abstractions of Duchamp-Villon, Arp and Brancusi, and anticipate many of the formal concerns of twentieth-century sculpture, even while his fascination with the formal problems of the human body links him with so much of the history of western art since Antiquity. Maillol's art is firmly rooted in the past, reveals many of the concerns of his present, and anticipates the future course of sculpture. This is not a unique situation, but it does demonstrate the creative power of much of his art. Only the greatest artists can use tradition for their own purposes, without being stifled by it. Maillol's ability to do precisely that is demonstrated by the large sculpture. Through his efforts in the 1890s, he evolved the basis upon which he could expand his personal vision in the statues created after 1905.

Epilogue

The Large Sculpture

Maillol's paintings and tapestries have been situated within the widespread Postimpressionist reaction to Impressionism of the 1890s. Both the formal and iconographic vocabulary as well as the basic theoretical foundation of the large sculpture is based upon concepts which evolved among the avant-garde painters of the 1890s. All Maillol's work created during the first half of that decade must be understood and interpreted in the context of Nabi-Synthetist art theories. His large-scale sculpture may be viewed as the most significant sculptural expression of this movement within the avant garde which developed into neoclassicism by the late 1890s.

Most critics, with the exception of Denis, have tended to minimize the importance of his presculptural works, and have therefore provided interpretations of the large sculpture which are incomplete. Although a work of art is created ten or twenty years after a movement has "passed" in art-historical terms, it does not mean that the force of those concepts or models has ceased to be important for a creative artist. Especially in Maillol's case, his contacts with Denis and other Nabi painters only intensified in the years after 1900. Therefore, their ideas would be more active, if anything, upon his creations. The roots and the meaning of Maillol's later sculpture are to be found in the 1890s. The connections between these portions of the oeuvre is the subject of this discussion.

In the preceding chapter, it was noted that Maillol used two basic body types as alternative canons. *The Spring* (fig. 34) and the *Standing Bather* (fig. 35) were the examples cited to demonstrate them. The slender figure of the latter piece will resurface most obviously in the *Monument to Cézanne* (1925) and *Air* (Gug. 107, 1938), and in a less elongated form in *Flora* (Gug. 67, 1910). It was precisely this slender form which he chose for *Eve* (Gug. 25, 1899). However, after 1900, the thicker, heavier form of *The Spring* definitely dominates his oeuvre. One sees it in *Pomona* (Gug. 63, 1910), *Draped Bather* (1921) and *Venus* (Gug. 72, 1918-28), to cite just a few examples. Maillol does not invent his female type after 1900. He explores its potential and modifies it in hundreds of subtle ways in each new statue.

Maillol's vocabulary of poses for his large sculpture also rests firmly on his works from the 1890s. The eighteen statues donated by Mme. Vierny to the state, now in the Tuileries, is a representative group of his works. The positions of only a few statues cannot be traced back to a statuette, painting or tapestry created before 1905, or one based very closely upon a work created before that date. *Night* (Gug. 43) and *Action in Chains* (Gug. 52) are original positions created between 1905 and 1910. Only the position in the *Monument to Cézanne* and its sister statue the *Monument to the Dead* of *Port-Vendres* were created after 1910.[1]

The statuette *Small Seated Woman with Chignon* (Gug. 56) provides us with a very clear link between the paintings and tapestries and the later sculpture. For her position, Maillol reached back to one of his earliest paintings, *Girl Tending Cows* (fig. 2). The figure is in an almost identical position to the painted one, but the left arm does not rest upon the upraised knee, and the right leg is tucked under her, not stretched out. However, this pose had been used much more recently for the princess in *Music for a Bored Princess* (fig. 26). One need only point the right hand toward the body to see the same form. *Small Seated Woman with Chignon* is also very similar to the kneeling figures on the lids of the fountains and the carved wooden bas-relief, *Figure in a Meditative Pose* (fig. 29).

This statuette is clearly not the definitive form for a sculpted seated figure. Maillol later abandoned the fussy interest in drapery folds across the breast and between the legs in his mature works. If one compares *Small Seated Woman with Chignon* with *Crouching Woman with Pointed Chignon* (Gug. 28), there are very few differences, except the nudity of the latter work. From this statuette to the *Study for The Mediterranean* (Gug. 47) only a few changes are involved in the position of the figure: left arm bent and supported on her upraised knee and the right leg tucked into the opening of the left leg. Hackelsberger[2] has attributed these changes in position, correctly I believe, to the influence of Gauguin's image, *Aha Oe Feii?*.[3] The pose is given an expression of profound sadness in the *Monument to the Dead at Ceret, La Douleur* (1921-23), and the *Monument to Debussy* (Gug. 89, 1930). Finally the basic position is used again with some modifications in *The Mountain* (Gug. 98, 1937).

I have traced the development of this single form in some detail because it provides a very clear and typical example of the way Maillol creates. *The Mediterranean* is not the same figure as the girl in the Kansas painting, but it is the end point of a development that begins with that painting. Through a series of adjustments, large or small, one arrives, through an evolutionary process, at a sculptural masterpiece. Significantly, and most characteristically, this development often begins with a two-dimensional image from the 1890s. It is also very revealing that the definitive adjustments in the position of *The*

Mediterranean come from an image by Gauguin. Maillol remained faithful to the master who had been so important to his career as a painter.[4]

Another pose which recurs in Maillol's oeuvre is the standing figure, legs placed together, with the right knee slightly bent. The head looks forward, the right arm is turned back to the shoulder, and the left arm is extended down, against the leg. Drapery hangs down the back, not obscuring any of the anatomy, but forming a backdrop to the nude body. This pose was used first in the painting *The Mediterranean* (fig. 15). It recurs in *The Standing Bather* (ca. 1900) (fig. 36).[5] We see it again in a plaster statuette, *Young Girl Bathing*,[6] later cast into bronze, and the definitive version of the pose is the lifesize *Draped Bather* (1921). Maillol also used the position for the male figure of the *Cyclist* (Gug. 61, 1907).

One can make another grouping of Maillol statues based upon the figure in the *The Mediterranean* (fig. 15), if one ignores the position of the figure's arms, focusing only upon the upright body with the slightly bent knee. Maillol's torso of *Venus* is placed in essentially the same pose as the painted figure. Rewald established that the form of the body was based upon a statuette dated around 1903, close chronologically to the period under discussion. The bodies of three other large-scale statues, *Pomona* (1910), *Summer* (Gug. 64, 1910), *The Nymph* (1930) and, consequently, *The Three Nymphs* (Gug. 97, 1930-37) are positioned similarly.

The recurrence of each of these basic poses should not imply a process of mechanical repetition. They certainly do not look alike; each one has its own identity and is an original, unique creation. But their individuality derives from adjustments of anatomy and proportions, rather than from the basic position in which the figure is placed. One is dealing with beautiful variations on a theme.

There are many other examples of images adapted from a two-dimensional medium into sculpture. The pose of the central figure drawn on the basin of Fountain II is seen again in the *Standing Bather* (fig. 35). In the painting *Two Bathers* (fig. 17), the figure on the right is positioned in profile with one arm extended downwards behind her body. *Ile de France* (Gug. 82, 83) also has her arms extended behind her body, and is in a similar walking stance. The close correspondence between the cartoons for Maillol's last, uncompleted tapestry and the relief *Desire* (Gug. 51, 1906-08) has been noted above.

By contrast to the procedure discussed above, in several later works a new sculpture was created by an alteration of position only. For example, Maillol rearranged a cut plaster cast of the *Monument to Cézanne* to make *Air*. The conception of this work is described by Rewald:

The central figure of this monument, a large reclining nude, does not measure less than three meters in length. The artist used for this project an old study scarcely ten centimeters in size, and representing a nude girl extended, carried away, as if by a whirlwind, abandoning her supple limbs to the breeze (Gug. 31). Inspired by this clay sketch, Maillol had the idea to cut a large plaster of the monument to Cézanne and to build the figure of *Air* with these elements.

Again, Maillol is reaching back to one of his images created around 1900 for his initial inspiration. *The River* was evolved by cutting a plaster cast of *The Mountain,* changing the position of the limbs but not the anatomical structure. The *Pomone with Lowered Arms* (1937) is an adaptation of the original statue (1910), in which the arms extended at right angles to the body.

The conclusion should be clear. Maillol's work during the 1890s and early 1900s provided the basis, the fertile creative soil, which nurtured the growth of the remarkably beautiful large-scale bronzes and marbles of the 1910s, 1920s, and 1930s. Not only did Maillol find the source of inspiration for the forms and poses for so many of his large-scale sculpture in works executed during that period, as indicated above, but also the philosophical system for the sculpture was evolved directly out of ideas developed by a number of artists, and articulated by Maurice Denis, in collaboration, at times, with Symbolist writers and poets during the 1890s.

In chapter 2 certain basic Nabi doctrines were discussed in connection with Maillol's paintings. To understand fully the impact of the 1890s on Maillol's sculpture, it is necessary to examine Maillol's own statements expressing his theoretical orientation to his sculpture and relate them to Nabi theories and Denis's ideas on classical art, formulated after 1898.

As noted above, around 1890, it was necessary to assert that the work of art was an independent creation with its own laws and rules. In later years, Maillol frequently articulated similar beliefs. He also believed that art was not a copy of nature and made this idea the guiding concept for his works:

What is difficult is to escape from nature.[8] It is not sufficient to have a model and copy it: nothing is simpler. Without doubt, nature is the base of work.... But art does not consist in copying nature.[9]

According to Nabi theories, the Synthesis was an important method for achieving the proper deformation from nature and establishing the desired classical balance between the artist's own feelings and reality. Maillol was very conscious of the importance of maintaining a synthetic vision in his sculpture. (We have seen him do just that in his paintings and tapestries.) Exclusively in the form of the female body, Maillol sought to express the unity and beauty of nature. Through his generalized nudes he could describe the underlying similarities of forms in nature: the "correspondences," in Baudelaire's term, beneath the superficial diversity of things in the world around us. An examination of some of his statements on the subject will clarify Maillol's personal interpretation of the term:

> It is necessary to be synthetic. We were naturally so when we were young, just like the African sculptors who condensed twenty forms into one. The figures of Maurice Denis were composed of two or three lines and an agreeable color, and by these simplifications, he gave an element of freshness, of youth, of tenderness in the composition to all modern painting. We are in an era when it is necessary to put many things into a synthesis.[11]

Maillol clearly understood that a piece of sculpture was a symbol, and should not describe only one piece of nature:

> The portrait and the statue are, for me, completely opposite things.[12]

> The particular is not interesting. If I copied Dina in this statue, it would only be Dina, it would be nothing. That is a facility.... What interests me, what I seek, is the general. This is so that my statue represents an idea.... These legs, if I copy them, they would only be Dina's legs.... What I wish, is to give them style.[13]

Maillol did not make many portraits, but the *Bust of Renoir* (1907) shows a very different approach to form than any of the works from the 1890s or the large sculpture. Its surface is craggy, with broken contours, a very specific physiognomy, with sharp angles of hat and cheek. It is a very lively and vivid portrayal of a specific person. This contrasts quite clearly with the very simple, almost geometrically pure solid forms which dominate the large-scale sculpture.

The ability to render a synthetic image is a basic characteristic of all classical artists. Denis defined this aspect of Maillol's art as "The Classical Gift":

> The ideal in Art is to condense, to summarize in a small number of clear and concise forms the infinitely varied connections which we perceive in Nature. It is to reduce to the essential our most particular sensations, it is to make something simple from the complicated.... In the notion of classical art, what dominates, thus, is the idea of synthesis.[14]

Maillol has definitely reduced his creations to the small number of forms Denis specifies. As has been clearly demonstrated above, "It was characteristic of Maillol that he never felt the need for a great variety of poses in his works. In his sculpture and his graphic art, variations of the same pose, like the variations on a theme in music occur again and again."[15] Of course, limiting the subject of all of his works exclusively to the female form is in itself a synthetic device. Maillol provides us with additional information on the way in which he perceives these unities in a variety of natural forms:

All ascending lines in nature, all verticals are straight, all horizontals round. Let us take a tree trunk. Its verticals are straight as a candle. In carving it, there is almost nothing but round forms. Carrying over this principle, which I have found in nature to the human figure, you will have the ground plan of my Aesthetic.[16]

Maillol believed in a uniform structural system for all organic objects in nature. He called it an "architecture": "I seek architecture and volumes. Sculpture is architecture and the equilibrium of the masses."[17]

This statement explains, perhaps, the reasons for the ubiquitous motif of the tree trunks in Maillol's paintings and tapestries. In those flat media, where it was physically impossible for him to make all horizontals round, he sought to insert an image of an object in nature which he perceived as closely related to the form of a young woman. Therefore, he provided over and over again a painted tree, usually set to one side of the composition, seeking to lead the viewer's perceptions toward the conclusions which he had reached through study and meditation.

This philosophy of art is ultimately based upon the belief that there exists a reality truer and closer to God beneath, behind or above the superficial appearances of objects in this world: "We insisted on this idea, that the visible is the manifestation of the invisible, that forms, colors are the signs of our states of soul."[18] Reality or the sensual information from the physical world is of importance to the artist only in so far as he can use that data to distinguish the Idea in the Platonic sense which hovers behind the tangible manifestations of our consciousness and then to express his emotional reactions to that "reality." These concepts, which originated with Plotinus, have a long history of modifications. Schopenhauer was the first to revive them in the beginning of the nineteenth century, and, in the later part of the century they had many spokesmen.

Nabi doctrine was largely based on these fundamental concepts, and the direct source for the group theoretician, Sérusier, was Baudelaire. Sérusier had described his ideas on reality:

Nature... merely supplies us with inert materials. A human mind alone can arrange them in such a way that, through them, it can express its feelings and its thoughts by means of *correspondences*. That is how we arrive at style, the ultimate aim of all art.[19]

This idea is virtually identical to Baudelaire's concept of nature as a dictionary, and his theory of correspondences, and one must assume that Baudelaire's ideas influenced Sérusier.

In another article, Denis firmly connects Séreusier's doctrines to Neo-Platonism:

Symbolism was like Sérusier himself, neo-platonic; writers and painters fell into accord to affirm that natural objects are the signs of Ideas; that the visible is the manifestation of the invisible; that sounds, colors, words have a value . . . expressive outside of all representation, outside even of the literal sense of words. . . .

In order to justify these affirmations, the Symbolists critics called on Hegel, Swedenborg, Edgar Poe, Baudelaire."[20]

Thus in late nineteenth-century France, art which was reacting to Positivism borrowed a "distinctly German mystical attitude" upon which to build its theoretical framework.[21]

Maillol's stated goal for his sculpture is precisely that which Denis and Sérusier sought, i.e., to express the artist's preconceived Idea about nature, suffused by his emotions and his feelings toward the world. He expressed this clearly in the following statement:

Form pleases me and I make it, but for me, it is only the means to express the Idea. It is ideas which I seek. I use form to arrive at that which is without form. I am trying to speak of something which is not palpable, which one cannot touch. The idea must be preconceived. It is necessary to determine it before one sees the model.[22]

Maillol clearly believed in the Platonic system, and discussed this with John Rewald:

You understand, . . . for Plato idea and form were one, and that is also how I see it. Form and preconceived idea guide the artist. Force, grace and all the other elements are added in the course of creation and make the product not merely the materialization of an idea, of an intellectual concept, but a work of art.[23]

Although we have no statements from the early years to prove it, there is no reason to suppose that Maillol's goals for his art were any different during the period when he painted and made tapestries than they were during the years when he was a sculptor. At each phase of our analysis, the ways in which Maillol's paintings and tapestries reveal similar Synthetist-Symbolist concerns, have been analyzed.

That Maillol was pursuing a symbolic image in his sculpture cannot be doubted. His success in this aspect varied from piece to piece. For this writer, *The Mediterranean* is the most successful attempt in sculpture of the integration of form with symbol. One cannot be fooled into seeing this piece of sculpture only as a beautiful woman, as one can with some of the later works. One must interpret it symbolically. Yet the work maintains its allegiance to the visible world by existing on the level of being a clearly recognizable woman. The parts of the body have been abstracted so that each unit is clearly defined. All chance details have been eliminated. Each part is essential to the structure of the whole.[24] We can therefore observe the balance between nature and the artist's modification of natural forms observed with a classical equilibrium. *The Mediterranean* not only symbolizes all women, but also encompasses within her contours, convexities and concavities the suggestion of a variety of inanimate objects: trees, rocks, mountains, bays. In this work, Maillol has achieved the goal of expressing an Idea clothed in a tangible form.

It was noted above that the final position of *The Mediterranean* is derived from Gauguin's *Aha Oe Feii?* (W. 461). The similarities penetrate beyond formal correspondences:

> The relation between the *Mediterranean* and Gauguin's *Aha Oe Feii?* . . . is close, not only in the posture and the simplified modelling of the limbs, but in the expression. Both works project an atmosphere of close communion between human beings and the earth which nourishes them. Maillol's figure is as much a metaphor of the cultural geography invoked by the title he later gave her as Gauguin's Tahitians are inseparable from the nature which surrounds and supports them. . . . [25]

As Maillol ages and moves away from the atmosphere of discovery in his art, his treatment of anatomy moves in two directions. We can establish *The Mediterranean* as a standard for a successful combination of natural forms and inorganic abstraction. In his later work, the balance is upset; we see either an increased naturalism or a rather coarse neoclassical abstraction. An example of the former tendency would be *Harmony* (Gug. 111), which was created in the presence of the model, Dina Vierny. Although the form of the body does not exactly mimic the model's, it does possess a greater organic unity, a fluidity which matches reality much more closely than the form of *The Mediterranean*. An example of the latter tendency, i.e., a coarse neoclassicism, would be the *Monument to the Dead at Banyuls* and *Girl Seated,*[26] both from the 1930s. These works display a lifelessness, a use of formulae rather than a fresh sculptural statement. In this writer's opinion, they are among Maillol's least successful works.

Finally, one must ask, "What do they mean?" The nonspecific nature of Maillol's sculpture has permitted a wide variety of interpretations in the literature. I believe that Maillol's conception of sculpture is founded upon the concepts articulated by Denis, as spokesman for the Nabis, and cannot be understood except in terms of the goals for art sought by that Postimpressionist generation. Maillol wanted to create an artistic expression which would be founded upon reality (in his case, the reality of the female body) but which would transcend that reality to create an image that would express abstract, nonspecific ideas and emotions.

He discovered in himself a natural facility, a gift for sculpting the female body, which expressed both his feelings toward all women and all of nature, in one fundamental form that could be modified at will. (In Maillol's two-dimensional works, he had to divide his images into two component parts—the vegetal, i.e., the landscape, and the human, i.e., the female figure, thus diluting the impact.)

Maillol, as Mme. Vierny rightly insists, was striving for a personal form of perfection. I believe he first wanted to create beautiful sculpture worthy of long contemplation: statues which would be sufficiently nonspecific so that the viewer would be forced to relate the sculptured image to other women, landscape elements, and a variety of natural phenomena. Maillol wanted to share his personal love for the countryside, i.e., nature uncontaminated by man, with his viewer. To achieve this goal, he chose the medium of the female body. He wanted his works to be open to a variety of possible interpretations so that the viewer would be forced to participate in the "creative act,"[27] rather than have the meaning programmed for him as it was in so much nineteenth-century academic sculpture. With these works, the viewer has the freedom to interpret from his own perspective, his own experience.

Maillol's art, as Denis so correctly perceived, is based upon the Synthesis. By synthesizing many different forms into one piece of sculpture, the possibilities of interpretation expand rapidly. Maillol's sculptures were designed to mean many things; to convey a range of emotions—grief, love, thought, sadness, beauty, life. And very often one may read two, three, or more emotions into a Maillol sculpture all at once. In their simplicity, they are bursting with "meaning." They require only a sensitive viewer to "hear" them speak.

Appendix

Catalogue Raisonné of the Tapestries

1. *Girls in a Park*, 1893. (fig. 21)
   Collection: Dina Vierny
   Exhibitions: Paris, Salon de la Société Nationale des Beaux-Arts, 1893
   Salon de la Libre Esthétique, Brussels, 1894
   References: Gauguin, *Essais d'Art Libre*, February-March-April, 1894
   The history of this piece is recorded in Cladel, (*Aristide Maillol*, p. 54) and in Dr. Bassères's diary (Puig, "Aristide Maillol," p. 15). It was originally sold for 300 francs to a man from Marseilles, probably M. Archbold Aspol, whose name is listed as the owner in the catalogue of the Salon de la Libre Esthétique, in 1894. Thirty years later, it was acquired by the Galerie Druet, where Maillol purchased it himself for 6000 francs.
   Howaldt mentions that the quality of the execution is unsteady and not always satisfactory. ("Bildteppiche der Stilbewegung," pp. 50-51.)

2. *The Enchanted Garden*, 1894. (fig. 22)
   190 X 105 cm.
   Collection: Dina Vierny
   Sewn in bottom center: Aristide Maillol
   Exhibitions: La Libre Esthétique, 1894, "Broderie" Solomon R. Guggenheim Museum, *Aristide Maillol: 1861-1944*, New York, 1975, no. 8
   Illustrations: Howaldt, "Bilteppiche der Stilbewegung," p. 64. Chevalier, *Maillol*, p. 10 (color detail) Solomon R. Guggenheim Museum, *Aristide Maillol: 1861-1944*, New York, 1975, p. 39

3. *Young Women in a Park*, ca. 1895. (fig. 23)
   180 X 180 cm.
   Collection: M. Philippe Gangnat
   Exhibitions: Hamburg, 1961-62
   Illustrations: Rewald, *Post-Impressionism*, p. 470
   Young Women in a Park shows a group of seven women. Three are seated on a bench which is positioned on a diagonal, while four are seated on the ground, opposite them. The woman closest to the viewer, seated on the bench, holds an open book from which she reads to the group. Maillol used a similar motif in another tapestry, *The Book* (1896) (fig. 24).
   John Rewald dates this work "ca. 1893." At the Maillol retrospective in Hamburg in 1962, it was dated "um 1894." Howaldt believes it predates *Music* (fig. 25), placing it between 1894-95 and 1897-98. It is quite possible that this work is the tapestry Maillol exhibited in 1895 at the Société Nationale des Beaux Arts, no. 295. However, it is also possible that this work is a tapestry called *The Garden*, which was exhibited in 1899 at the same Salon, no. 288. It was

again displayed at Maillol's first one-man show in 1902, and listed as belonging to a M. Léo Rouanet. As we do not know the provenance of this tapestry, it is difficult to determine which tapestry it actually is.

Sylistic factors favor the earlier date of 1895. Howaldt's main reason for an earlier date rests upon the dress styles. *Young Women in a Park* shows Maillol's concern for the billowing folds of skirts, also apparent in *The Enchanted Garden.* In *Music,* the next executed tapestry, the dresses are much simpler and reveal the form of the bodies beneath. This factor, combined with the overly crowded composition argues for a date before the execution of *La Musique* (1896-97), i.e., 1895.

4.   *The Book,* ca. 1895. (fig. 24)
Present whereabouts unknown, originally acquired by Maurice Bouchor from the artist
Exhibitions: Salon de la Société Nationale des Beaux-Arts, Paris, 1896, no. 321
Paris, 1902
Paris, 1911, no. 81
The composition was reproduced by Maillol, in a woodcut: Guerin, no. 3 (fig. 57). Since Maillol made a woodcut of *Music* which follows the composition of that tapestry exactly, this woodcut is a reliable source for the appearance of *The Book.* The use of a reader and a group of listeners relates this tapestry directly to *Young Women in a Park.*

5.   *Music* or *The Concert of Women,* 1896-97. (fig. 25)
155 X 204 cm.
Provenance: Commissioned by Princess Bibesco
Carmen Sylva
Museum of Decorative Arts, Copenhagen
Exhibitions: Paris, 1911, no. 80
Copenhagen, 1947
Paris, 1955, no. 210
Paris, 1961
The colors are derived from plant dyes and belong overwhelmingly to the green family. The tones range from gold-green to a deep blue-green. A small amount of red is used in the mandolins and there are an evenly dispersed variety of brown tones (ranging from red-brown to beige).[1]

There is a very constrained use of gold thread in this tapestry. One finds it only in the neck ruffle and sleeves of the central mandolin player. In fact, there is an overall plainness and simplicity which contrasts with the richly encrusted embroidery of *The Enchanted Garden.*[2]

Most of the stitches are one centimeter high. However, the stitching frequently follows and accents a contour. This gives the figures a drawn quality, which Lassen interprets as Maillol's attempt to imitate Gauguin's *cloisonisme.* Often yarns of different colors are alternated stitch by stitch, which Lassen believes is an attempt to explore the possibilities of expanding the textile palette, with a limited number of dyes.

Related Works: Maillol repeated this design in a lithograph (Guerin, no. 261). He also created a two-figure zincograph in a variation on this theme (Guerin, no. 260). It shows a very slim princess with long hair seated on the ground. A single mandolin player sits below and to her right. Her body is positioned in the same way as the central mandolin player of the tapestry.

The central musician is also reproduced in a bas-relief, carved in a round piece of wood.[3]

A complete oil sketch also exists for this tapestry.[4] The sketch agrees with the tapestry in all important respects and even has a border left blank.

6. *Music for a Bored Princess,* 1897. (fig. 26)
    164 X 178 cm.
    Collection: Museum of Decorative Arts, Copenhagen (donated by Princess Bibesco)
    Exhibitions: Paris, 1911, no. 83
    Copenhagen, 1947
    Paris, 1955
    Paris, 1961
    A cartoon for this tapestry is reproduced in Howaldt, ("Bildteppiche der Stilbewegung"). The figures are taller and given more graceful proportions. She feels that the cartoon more accurately represents Maillol's creative intentions. Lassen observes that the heads of the musicians, in their broad, open faces and piled hair, anticipate several of Maillol's later busts, e.g., Mme. Denis.
    The dresses of these figures are more severe than in *Music.* Here there is none of the flowing sleeves and swirling skirts of the earlier works. The skirt of the mandolin player on the right is a solid plane of color with four linear accents to relieve it. The indication of folds in the player on the left is also very restrained: they resemble decorative stripes, rather than volumetric folds.

7. *The Bather,* 1898-1900. (fig. 27)
    90 X 90
    Collection: Prince Antoine Bibesco
    Exhibitions: Paris, 1911, no. 84 (listed as "La Vague, écran")
    Paris, 1947, no. 220 (listed as "La Mer: exécutée au petit pointe par Mme. Maillol, 1895")
    Rewald, Lassen and Howaldt date this tapestry ca. 1902, but Hackelsberger believed it was created in the mid-1890s. It could not have been executed after 1902, since Howaldt says it was shown at Vollard's, and Maillol had ceased all activity in the medium by then. But it seems more logical to assume that the tapestry was created before 1900 when Maillol had purchased his loom. Therefore, I would date this work between 1898 and 1900.
    The body of the figure is basically a solid area of beige, with no internal modeling. Her profile is outlined with a dark brown line. A sewn line is used to trace the contour of her left leg. The water is indicated by large areas of blue and green. The white of the drapery stands out very brightly against the beige of her body. Folds are indicated by sewn lines of blue and small areas of alternating blue and white threads.

8. Tapestry for a Chair: *Dancer with a Scarf, Head to Head.*
    Collection: Antoine Bibesco
    Exhibitions: Paris, 1911, no. 85
    Illustrations: Rewald, *Aristide Maillol,* London, Paris, New York, 1939

9. Tapestry for a Chair: *The Scarf and the Baskets.*
    Collection: Antoine Bibesco
    Exhibition: Paris, 1911, no. 86
    Illustrations: Rewald, *Aristide Maillol,* London, Paris, New York, 1939

1. *Self Portrait (Portrait de l'artiste par lui-même)* (1888)

2. *Girl Tending Cows* (1890-91)

3. *Young Girl in Red: Portrait of Jeanne Sarrail* (1890)

4. *Woman with an Umbrella*
    (La Femme à l'ombrelle) (ca. 1891)

5. *Profile of a Woman (Profil de femme)* (1891)

6. *Profile of a Woman (Profil de femme)* (ca. 1891)

7. *Spring (Deux jeunes filles, Le Printemps)* (ca. 1892)

8. *Crowned Child (L 'Enfant couronné)* (ca. 1892)

9. *Two Girls (Les Deux jeunes filles)* ca. 1893

10. *Portrait of Mme. Maillol (Portrait de Mme. Maillol)*
(1894-95)

11. *Portrait of Mme. Maillol (Portrait de Mme. Maillol)*
(first version) (1894-95)

12. *Two Girls (Les Deux jeunes filles)* (1894-95)

13. *Bather Seated on White Drapery (Baigneuse assise sur un drap blanc)* (ca. 1895)

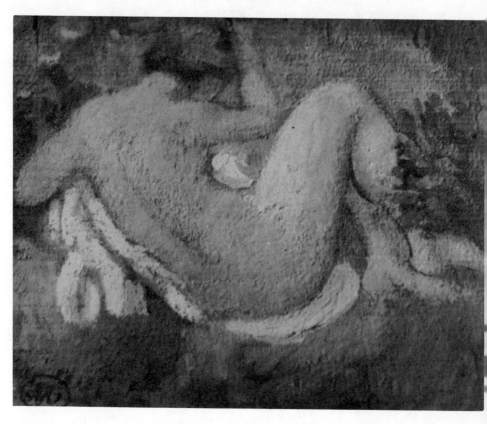

14. *The Wave (La Vague)* (1895-96)

15. *La Cote d-Azur or The Mediterranean* (1895-96)

16. *The Woman and the Wave (La Femme à la vague)* (1895-96)

17. *Two Bathers* (ca. 1896-97)

18. *Two Washerwomen (Les Lavandières)* (ca. 1896).

19. *Two Women* (over fireplace) (ca. 1896)

20. *Women Picking Pears at Pont Aven*
    (Femmes cueillant des poires à Pont Aven)
    (1888)

21. *Girls in a Park (Jeunes filles dans un parc)* (1893)

22. *The Enchanted Garden (Le Jardin enchanté)* (1894)

23. *Young Women in a Park* (ca. 1895)

24. *The Book (Le Livre)* (ca. 1895)

25. *Music or The Concert of Women* (1896-97) *(La Musique or Concert des femmes)*

26. *Music for a Bored Princess (Musique pour la Princesse qui s'ennuie)* (1897)

27. *The Bather (La Baigneuse)* (1898-1900)

28. *Two Girls (Les Deux jeunes filles)* (ca. 1900)

29. *Figure in a Meditative Pose* (ca. 1894)

30.   Mirror Frame (ca. 1896)

31. Headboard of a Crib (1896)

32. Fountain II (1897-1902)

33. Fountain III (1897-1902)

34. *La Source* or *The Spring* (1896)

35. *Bather* (1899)

36. *Standing Bather* (1900)

Notes

Introduction

1. Jeanne Stump, "Maillol in the 1890's," *The Register of the Museum of Art, University of Kansas* 4 (March 1971): 34-47.

2. Gabrielle Howaldt, "Bildteppiche der Stilbewegung," *Kunst in Hessen und am Mittelrhein, Schriften der Hessischen Museen,* no. 4 (1964).

3. MaryAnne Stevens, "Innovation and Consolidation in French Painting" in *Post-Impressionism: Cross-Currents in European Painting* (London, Royal Academy of Arts, 1979-80), p. 20.

4. Adrien Mithouard, "Le Classique occidental," *L'Occident,* vol. 1, no. 4 (March 1902), pp. 179-87.

5. Maurice Denis, "Aristide Maillol," *L'Occident* (November 1905) reprinted as a monograph, Paris: G. Crès: Collections de Cahiers d'Aujourd'Hui. 1925, and in *Théories 1890-1910: Du symbolism vers un nouvelle ordre classique,* Paris, Bibliotèque de l'Occident, 1913.

6. Royal Academy of Arts, London, *Post-Impressionism: Cross-Currents in European Painting,* 1979-80.

7. This translation, as well as all others in this book, are by the author. Maillol quoted in Henri Frère, *Conversations avec Maillol* (Geneva: P. Cailler, 1956), p. 304.

8. Judith Cladel, *Aristide Maillol: Sa vie, son oeuvre, ses idées* (Paris: Grasset, 1937).

9. Published with commentary by René Puig, "La Vie misérable et glorieuse d'Aristide Maillol," *Tramontane* 49, nos. 483-84 (1965): 1-52.

10. Maurice Denis, "Aristide Maillol."

11. Octave Mirbeau, "Aristide Maillol," *La Revue des Revues,* April 1905, republished as a monograph, Paris: Société des Dilettantes, 1921.

12. Waldemar-George, *Aristide Maillol,* trans. Diana Imber (Greenwich, Conn.: New York Graphic Society, 1965), second edition, 1977.

13. Marcel Guerin, *Catalogue raisonné de l'oeuvre gravé et lithographié d'Aristide Maillol,* 2 vols. (Geneva: P. Cailler, 1965).

14. Carola Giedion-Welcker, *Modern Plastic Art* (Zurich, Girsberger, 1937), p. 8.

15. Albert Elsen, *Origins of Modern Sculpture: Pioneers and Premises* (New York, George Braziller, Inc., 1974), p. 90.

Chapter 1

1. Judith Cladel, *Aristide Maillol: Sa vie, son oeuvre, ses idées* (Paris: Grasset, 1937).

2. René Puig, "La Vie misérable et glorieuse d'Aristide Maillol," *Tramontane* 49, nos. 483-84 (1965): 1-52.

3. Ibid., p. 9.

4. Reproduced in Marguette Bouvier, *Aristide Maillol* (Lausanne: Editions Marguerat, 1945), p. 29.

5. Cladel, *Aristide Maillol,* p. 14.

6. Ibid., p. 15.

7. Puig, "Aristide Maillol," p. 10.

8. Ibid., p. 11.

9. Ibid., p. 12.

10. Cladel, *Aristide Maillol,* p. 19.

11. Ibid., p. 20.

12. Ibid., p. 21.

13. AJ[52] 79, page 120ff. Maillol's total score was 87.60. The highest ranked applicant received 152.60 points. Maillol told Cladel that he was second to the last.

14. Puig, "*Aristide Maillol,"* p. 12.

15. Cladel, *Aristide Maillol,* p. 26.

16. Ibid., p. 28.

17. Ibid., p. 32.

18. Laugé worked in a conservative academic mode until 1888, when he returned to his native Toulouse. After this time, he changed his style under the influence of Seurat's Pointillism and painted for the rest of his life in a form of fractured brushstroke, which has been termed "virgulism," comma strokes of color rather than dots. Charles Pornon, introduction to the catalog, "A. Laugé et ses amis Maillol et Bourdelle" (Toulouse, 1961), p. 3.

19. Bourdelle worked as an assistant for Rodin from 1893 to 1900. His personal style and sculptural interests during this period can be easily surmised from this fact. It was only after 1900, when he had surely ceased to see Maillol, that he began to explore classicist themes, e.g., *The Dying Centaur* or *Heracles, Archer.* At this time he achieves a sort of frozen monumentality and smooth surfaces and contours which can be compared with Maillol's sculptural idiom.

20. Cladel, *Aristide Maillol,* p. 32.

21. In 1897 the Maillol ménage moved to the suburbs, for financial reasons. No doubt the friendship between the two wives helped to preserve their relationship. In June 1899, Mme. Maillol became the godmother of the Monfreid's daughter.

22. A drawing of a seated woman with a guitar is in the Monfreid collection. J. Loize, *De Maillol et Codet à Segalen: Les amitiés du peintre Georges-Daniel de Monfreid et ses reliques de Gauguin* (Paris: 1951), p. 20. Monfreid later wrote on the work, "Croquis par Maillol (quand

il habitait Rue de Sèvres)." Also a portrait sketch of Maillol by Monfreid, dated around 1886, is in the Monfreid collection. (Loize, Document No. 233.)

23. Since 1882 Monfreid had attended the Academie Collarossi, where he knew Emile Schuffenecker... Schuffenecker was a former colleague of Gauguin's at the Bertin bank. In late 1887, when Gauguin returned to Paris, "Schuff" fed and housed him. Loize, *De Maillol et Codet à Segalen,* p. 14.

24. Letter from Maillol to Denis, reprinted in Denis, *Journal* (Paris: La Colombe, 1957-59), 1:25.

25. Cladel, *Aristide Maillol,* p. 31.

26. Ibid., p. 35.

27. Ibid., p. 34.

28. John Rewald, *Aristide Maillol* (New York, Paris, London: Hyperion Press, 1939), p. 9.

29. Letter from Maillol to Denis, reprinted in Denis, *Journal,* 1:24.

30. The plays often had musical accompaniment. Ernst Chausson composed music for the *Tempest,* for example. The repertoire inclined towards metaphysical, spiritualistic themes. Bouchor published under his own name *La Dévotion à Saint André* in 1892 and *Les Mystères d'Eleusis* in 1894. Maillol was commissioned to paint the scenery for the later work, according to his own recollections.

31. Cladel, *Aristide Maillol,* pp. 42-43.

32. This entry was dated Jeudi, 4 Janvier, 1894, quoted in Loize, *De Maillol et Codet à Segalen,* p. 18.

33. Harry Kessler, *Souvenirs d'un Européen,* trans. Blaise Briod (Paris, 1936), entry for Sunday, June 13, 1926, p. 204.

34. Cladel, *Aristide Maillol,* p. 15.

35. Ibid., p. 57.

36. Ibid., p. 59.

37. It is generally repeated by scholars that Maillol met the young group of artists who called themselves the Nabis, i.e., the Hebrew word for prophet, in 1893.

38. Jozsef Rippl-Ronai came to Paris to study painting in 1889. He became acquainted with the Nabis, probably after his one-man show at the Pavillon of the Austrian Ambassador in March 1892. His strange, expressive style of painting was in line with the types of works being painted by the Nabis at that moment. We do not know how or when Maillol met Rippl-Ronai.

39. It was published in an obscure Hungarian journal, but a copy of the article was loaned to me from the personal archives of John Rewald.

40. George Mauner, *The Nabis: Their History and Their Art: 1888-1896* (New York and London, Garland Publishing Inc., 1978), p. 173.

41. Maurice Denis et al., *Aristide Maillol,* Cahiers Comoedia-Charpentier, November 1943, p. 8.

42. P. Bonnard in Bonnard et al., "Aristide Maillol," *Cahiers des amis de l'art,* no. 10 (Paris, 1946: p. 46.

43. This "was considered a practice crucial to the development of an artist's personal viewpoint, his originality." Albert Boime, *The Academy and French Painting in the Nineteenth Century* (London: Phaidon, 1971), p. 34.

44. They are now in the private collection of G. Jedlicka of Zurich.

45. Cladel, *Aristide Maillol,* p. 56.

46. Ibid., p. 61.

47. Puig, "Aristide Maillol," p. 18.

48. Mme. Harlor, "Maillol," *La Fronde,* June 26, 1902.

49. Mirbeau, "Aristide Maillol," p. 335.

Chapter 2

1. Mark Roskill, *Van Gogh, Gauguin and the Impressionist Circle* (Greenwich, Conn.: New York Graphic Society, 1970), p. 7.

2. Denis, "Préface de la IXe exposition des peintres impressionistes et symbolistes chez le Barc de Boutteville," reprinted in *Du symbolism au classicism: Théories,* ed. O. Revault d'Allones (Paris: Hermann, Miroirs de l'art, 1964), p. 48.

3. Albert Aurier, "Les Peintres symbolistes," *La Revue Encyclopédique,* April 1, 1892, reprinted in *Oeuvres Posthumes* (Paris, 1893), pp. 294-95.

4. Denis, "Les Arts à Rome ou le méthode classique," reprinted in *Théories 1890-1910: Du Symbolism et de Gauguin vers un nouvel ordre classique,* 3d ed. (Paris: Bibliotèque de l'Occident, 1913), p. 50.

5. Denis, "Définition du néo-traditionnalisme," *Art et Critique,* August 1890, reprinted in *Théories.*

6. Ibid., p. 267.

7. Denis, "Aristide Maillol," *Théories,* p. 228.

8. Ibid., p. 227.

9. Judith Cladel, *Aristide Maillol; Sa vie, son oeuvre, ses idées* (Paris: Grasset, 1939), p. 39.

10. Reproduced in Marguette Bouvier, *Aristide Maillol* (Lausanne: Editions Marguerat, 1945).

11. Cladel, *Aristide Maillol,* p. 38.

12. Cladel, *Aristide Maillol,* p. 37.

13. Albert Boime, *The Academy and French Painting in the Nineteenth Century* (London: Phaidon, 1971), pp. 122-23.

14. Cladel, *Aristide Maillol,* p. 24.

15. Ibid., p. 40.

16. Art Gallery of Ontario, Toronto, Canada, *Puvis de Chavannes and the Modern Tradition* (1975), catalogue by Richard J. Wattenmaker, pp. 23-24.

17. Charles Chassé, *The Nabis and their Period,* trans. Michael Bullock (New York: Praeger, 1969), p. 25.

18. John Rewald, *Aristide Maillol* (New York, Paris, London: Hyperion Press, 1939), p. 10.

19. Cladel, *Aristide Maillol,* p. 130.

20. Numbers in parentheses refer to the definitive catalogue of Gauguin's paintings by Georges Wildenstein, *Gauguin* (Paris: Les Beaux-Arts, 1964). In this connection, Stump also cites Wildenstein, nos. 203, 308, and 344. Jeanne Stump, "Maillol in the 1890's," *Register of the Museum of Art, Univ. of Kansas* 4 (March 1971), p. 47.

21. Roskill, *Van Gogh, Gauguin and the Impressionist Circle,* p. 132.

22. Another painting on display at the Café Volpini, *Dans les vagues* or *Ondine* greatly impressed Maillol, and he was to use the motif several years later for his composition *The Wave* (fig. 14). *Ondine* was one of the few large-scaled nudes painted by Gauguin prior to the Tahitian voyages. Maillol used *Ondine* for the woodcut which decorated the cover of the catalogue of the Volpini show, paired with a crouching figure and entitled *Aux Roches noirs.*

23. Stump, "Maillol in the 1890's," p. 36.

24. Richard Wattenmaker, *Puvis de Chavannes, and the Modern Tradition.* Calalogue, Art Gallery of Ontario, Toronto, Canada, 1975, p. 143.

25. Ibid.

26. Wendy Slatkin, "The Genesis of Maillol's *La Méditerranée*", *Art Journal,* XXXVIII, no. 3 (Spring, 1979), 184-89.

27. In the Burhle Collection, Zurich.

28. Quoted in George Mauner, *The Nabis, Their History and Their Art: 1888-96,* New York and London, Garland Publishing, Inc., 1978 (Ph.D. dissertation, Columbia University, 1966), p. 252.

29. Translated in: John House, "The Legacy of Impressionism in France" in *Post-Impressionism: Cross-Currents in European Painting* (London, Royal Academy of Arts, 1979-80), p. 17.

30. Roskill, *Van Gogh, Gauguin and the Impressionist Circle,* p. 48.

31. Quoted in Rewald, *Post-Impressionism: From Van Gogh to Gauguin,* 2d Ed. (New York: Museum of Modern Art, 1962), p. 211.

32. Cladel, *Aristide Maillol,* p. 39.

33. Denis, "Maillol," *Théories,,* p. 228.

34. Félix Fénéon, "La VIIIe exposition impressionniste," reprinted in Fénéon, *Au-delà de l'Impressionnisme,* ed. Françoise Cachin (Paris: Hermann, Miroirs de l'art, 1966), p. 67.

35. I would like to thank Dr. Paul Watson for bringing this to my attention.

36. John Rewald, "Maillol Remembered" (New York, The Solomon R. Guggenheim Museum, 1975), p. 12.

37. Cladel, *Aristide Maillol,* p. 3.

38. Present whereabouts unknown.

39. Numbers prefaced by "Gug." refer to the exhibition catalogue *Aristide Maillol: 1861-1944* (New York, Solomon R. Guggenheim Museum, 1975).

40. Denis, "Définition du néo-traditionnalisme," reprinted in *Théories,* p. 12.

41. Christopher Gray, *Sculpture and Ceramics of Paul Gauguin* (Baltimore: Johns Hopkins University Press, 1963), pp. 43-44.

42. Mauner, *The Nabis,* p. 225.

43. La belle fille sans souci qui laissait voir,
    En dansant, le secret blanc de sa gorge pure...
    L'Artifice joli d'un léger désespoir...
    C'est dans ton âme, beau chanteur, qu'elle dansait
    Selon les rites inconnu encore—et c'est
    Elle pour Muse que tes rimes ont choisie...
    La belle fille était comme ta fantaisie.

44. The French were only following the example of their British contemporaries in their idealization of women. The English painters of the second half of the nineteenth century worshipped an idealized female type, originated by Rosetti's choice of Lizzy Siddal. Throughout the century, the Aesthetic movement manifested its dreams and desires through images of women.

45. Mauner, *The Nabis,* p. 225.

46. Ibid., p. 229.

47. Ibid., p. 252.

48. Roskill, *Van Gogh, Gauguin and the Impressionist Circle,* p. 54.

49. In March 1891, Signac organized a retrospective exhibition at the Salon des Indépendants. In April 1891, Bernard mounted a show at the Gallery of the Barc de Boutteville. (Maillol was to exhibit there in 1896.)

50. Denis, "Définition du néo-traditionnalisme" in *Théories,* p. 1, translated in Herschel B. Chipp, *Theories of Modern Art* (Berkeley, Los Angeles and London, University of California Press, 1968), p. 94.

51. Roskill, *Van Gogh, Gauguin and the Impressionist Circle,* p. 14.

52. This motif appears in *Arearea (The Red Dog)* (W. 468), dated 1892; *E Haere Oe I Hia,* dated 1892 (W. 478); and *Ea Haere Ia Oe* (W. 501) in the Hermitage Museum, Leningrad.

53. Certainly, Maillol could have seen a variety of Denis's works without having met him personally since Denis was regularly exhibiting, after 1891, at both the Barc de Boutteville and the Salon des Indépendants.

54. Cladel, *Aristide Maillol,* p. 66.

55. Denis, quoted in Bernard Dorival, *Les Etapes de la Peinture Française,* 3 vols. (Paris: Gaillimard, 1946), 1:118.

56. This painting was not purchased by the state until 1895, but it had entered the public collections a short while before November 1893, when a color reproduction was published in the *Gazette des Beaux Arts.* Gustave Gruyer, "Vittore Pisano," *Gazette des Beaux Arts,* 3d period, 10 (November 1893): 366.

57. Reproduced in Rewald, *Aristide Maillol* (1939), plate 35.

58. The pastel in the Vierny collection is virtually identical to the work reproduced in Rewald (present whereabouts unknown), and the figure is turned in the opposite direction. Therefore, one can safely assume that the Vierny work was the one to which Maillol was referring. With the passage of time, he simply forgot that the "original" was a pastel, and not an oil.

59. Frère,*Conversations avec Maillol,* (Geneva: P. Cailler, 1956), p. 136.

60. Wildenstein no. 411.

61. René Puig, "La Vie misérable et glorieuse d' Aristide Maillol," *Tramontane* 49, nos. 483-84 (1965), p. 14.

62. It is painted on the reverse side of the oil sketch for the tapestry *La Musique.*

63. Now in the National Gallery, Washington, D.C.

64. Cladel, *Aristide Maillol,* p. 58.

65. Ibid., p. 38.

66. In the collection of Mme. Jacquart.

67. Tyson Collection, Philadelphia Museum of Art.

68. Wildenstein, no. 336, dated 1889.

69. This painting was sold to Jacques-Emile Blanche, shortly after its completion. Blanche sold it to Tyson in 1928. It is now in the Philadelphia Museum of Art, Tyson Collection. As mentioned above it was exhibited at the Galerie Durand-Ruel in May 1892 when Maillol could surely have seen it.

70. Vierny Collection.

71. Marcel Guerin, *Catalogue raisonné de l'oeuvre gravé et lithographié d'Aristide Maillol,* (Geneva: P. Cailler, 1965), no. 9.

72. Dorival, *Les Etapes de la Peinture Française,* 1:133-34.

73. This painting was exhibited at the Galerie Durand-Ruel, in November 1893.

74. Wayne Andersen, *Gauguin's Paradise Lost* (New York: Viking Press, 1971), p. 174.

75. Published by F. et P. Piranesi, Frères, with commentary by Louis Petit Radel, 2 vols.

76. W: 362, illustrated in Rewald, *The History of Impressionism,* 4th ed. (New York: Museum of Modern Art, 1973), p. 555. Collection Henry Ford II, Grosse Pointe, Michigan.

77. The way in which the Japanese depict waves had been accurately described: "The meanders of the current are written, the fringes of the wave drawn: this is the typical character of far-eastern prints—of which the *Mangwa,* among others, offer many examples. The Japanese applied themselves, because of their artistic traditions, to synthesize, to schematise, ... the diverse movements of the waters, sleeping or boiling currents." Yvonne Thirion, "De l'Influence de l'estampe japonaise sur la peinture française dans le séconde moitié du XIXe siècle (MS thesis, Paris), p. 122.

78. Guerin, no. 263.

79. Courbet's painting was in a private collection until 1893, when Durand Ruel bought it. It is now in the collection of the Metropolitan Museum, New York.

80. Loize, *De Maillol et Codet à Ségalen,* p. 56.

81. Frère, *Conversations avec Maillol,* pp. 135-36.

82. The parents of the present owner, Mme. Littaye-Belle, commissioned the fresco cycle.

83. This aspect of Maillol's personality was stressed by both Mr. John Rewald and Mme. Dina Vierny, independently, in conversations with the author.

Chapter 3

1. Judith Cladel, *Aristide Maillol: Sa vie, son oeuvre et ses idées* (Paris: Grasset, 1937), pp. 45-46.

2. Ibid., p. 49.

3. Gabriele Howaldt, "Bildteppiche der Stilbewegung," *Kunst in Hessen und am Mittelrhein: Schriften der Hessischen Museen* (Darmstadt, no. 4, 1964), p. 48. ["Die bedeutendsten französischen Bildteppiche jener Stilepoche um die Jahrhundertwende."].

4. Agnès Humbert, *Les Nabis et leur époque* (Geneva: P. Cailler, 1954), p. 8.

5. Jan Verkade was closely associated with the Nabis for a period of several years, around 1890. He later entered the monastery of Beuron. Jan Verkade, *Le Tourment de Dieu* (Paris: 1923), p. 94.

6. Rosalinde Bacou, "Décors d'appartements au temps des Nabis," *Art de France* 4 (1964): 191.

7. Gauguin, quoted in Merete Bodelsen, "The Missing Link in Gauguin's Cloisonism," *Gazette des Beaux Arts*, ser. 6, 53 (May-June 1959): 341.

8. In that year, Morris discussed the qualities of a good tapestry designer with Thomas Wardle. Martin Harrison and Bill Waters, *Burne-Jones* (London: Putnam, 1973), p. 137.

9. Jacques Lethève, "La Connaissance des Pré-Raphaélites anglaises en France: 1885-1900," *Gazette des Beaux-Arts*, ser. 6, 53 (May-June 1959): 315.

10. William Morris, *Textiles—Part I*, introductory notes to the catalogue of the first exhibition of the Arts and Crafts Society (London: Arts and Crafts Society, First Exhibition Catalogue, 1888).

11. Blanc, the founder of the *Gazette des Beaux Arts* was one of the most important conservative critics of the Second Empire. He had a very active career: he was director of Fine Arts under the Second Republic, and again in 1870. His book, *Grammaire des arts du dessin*, published in 1867, was influential for the Postimpressionists. Roskill has established that Van Gogh, Gauguin, and Seurat were all familiar with Blanc's writings on color "which made a great deal of Delacroix's colour practice." (Roskill, *Van Gogh, Gauguin and the Impressionist Circle*, p. 91.) In 1882, Blanc published the companion volume to the work cited above, *Grammaire des arts décoratifs.*

12. Charles Blanc, *Grammaire des arts décoratifs* (Paris: 1882), p. 94.

13. Henri Frère, *Conversations avec Maillol* (Geneva: P. Cailler, 1950), pp. 187-88.

14. Blanc, *Grammaire des arts décoratifs*, p. 99.

15. Ibid., p. 118.

16. There were a number of books about tapestries published in the 1880s. But virtually all were histories of the medium, tracing the technical and stylistic development of tapestries from the Middle Ages to the present. Jules Guiffrey's *Histoire de la Tapisserie depuis le Moyen Age jusqu'à nos jours* (Tours: Alfred Mame et fils, 1886); *La Tapisserie* by E. Müntz (Paris: Bibliothèque de l'enseignement des Beaux Arts, 1882); and a lavish two volume work by J.M.J. Guiffrey, E. Müntz, and A. Pinchart, *Histoire de la Tapisserie en France*, 2 vols. (Paris: Société anonyme de publications périodiques, 1878-85) are the most extensive texts which fall into this category. Only Blanc's text provided a set of guidelines for the tapestry designer, and for this reason would have been more valuable to Maillol than these other books.

17. This work is now in the Hessisches Landesmuseum, Darmstadt. It was commissioned by le Comte Antoine de la Rochefoucauld. Bernard also executed a lithograph (Collection M. Bernard Fort) and a stained glass window (now in Lille) of the same design (illustrated in John Rewald, *Post-Impressionism: From Van Gogh to Gauguin* (2nd ed., New York: Museum of Modern Art, 1962 , p. 197.)

18. It is probable that Gauguin encouraged Bernard to experiment with tapestries in a modern idiom since Gauguin himself was interested in tapestries as early as 1883. In a letter to his son, Lucien, Pisarro states that Gauguin tried to encourage him to create designs for "impressionist" tapestries [John Rewald, ed. *Camille Pisarro: Letters to his Son Lucien,* trans. Lionel Abel (New York: Pantheon Books, 1943), letter dated June 16, 1883].

19. Bernard's system is more exact, executed on a grid plan, while stitches in Maillol's tapestries tend to vary in length and to follow the outline of the form they are defining.

20. Maurice Denis, "Aristide Maillol," in *Théories* (Paris: Bibliotèque de l'Occident, 1913), p. 227.

21. Peter Selz states that "as early as 1890 Ranson made cartoons for tapestries which were executed in embroidery by his wife... " [Peter Selz, *Art Nouveau—Art and Design at the Turn of the Century* (New York: Museum of Modern Art, 1959), p. 58.] Unfortunately it is not possible to confirm this rather early date of 1890. (Personal communiqué, Mme. Michel Ranson.) The cartoon for *Tiger in the Jungle* was exhibited in 1893 at the Société des Artistes Independants. A lithography of the same subject is also dated 1893, which is the earliest firmly dated tapestry design. (Information provided by L. Clarice Davis, dissertation in progress, UCLA.)

22. Located in the Musée National d'Art Moderne, Paris.

23. Howaldt dates the design "um 1890," p. 46.

24. Cladel, *Aristide Maillol,* p. 46.

25. Ibid., p. 139.

26. Ibid.

27. Denis, "Définition du néo-traditionnalisme," reprinted in *Théories,* p. 12.

28. Personal communication from Mme. Geneviève Souchal, curator of the Musée de Cluny, author of the exhibition catalogue, *Chefs-d'oeuvres de la Tapisserie du XIVe au XVIe,* Paris, 1973.

29. The history of the garden motif in its religious and secular aspects is explored fully in Roberta S. Favis, "The Garden of Love in Fifteenth Century Netherlandish and German Engravings: Some studies in secular iconography in the late Middle Ages and Early Renaissance" (Ph.D. dissertation, University of Pennsylvania, 1974). This is my source for this information.

30. Raimond Van Marle, *Iconographie de l'Art Profane,* 2 vols. (The Hague: M. Nijhoff, 1931-32), 2:426.

31. Fashion magazines have been shown to be significant influences on both Cézanne and Monet in the 1860s and early 1870s. See Mark Roskill, "Early Impressionism and the Fashion Print," *Burlington Magazine* 112 (June 1970): 391-95.

32. Although Maillol told Bassères that it was his first work, Cladel does mention a tapestry which was sold to the Comte d'Esmont, who owned a villa at Fécamp. Of this supposed

earlier work, we have the following comment: "Gauguin did not deem it successful, because 'in tapestry, one should not use perspective.' " (Cladel, *Aristide Maillol*, p. 53.) Unfortunately, there is no corroborating evidence and no trace of a tapestry to support Cladel's statement, that this work preceded *Girls in a Park*.

33.   Puig publishes the following entry in Monfreid's diary without a specific date: "Passed by Bon Marché to buy wools for Maillol. Sent the wools to Banyuls." (René Puig, *"La Vie misérable et glorieuse d'Aristide Maillol,"* *Tramontane* 49, nos. 483-84, (1965), p. 15.) Loize also mentions this entry, but places it in the winter of 1895. (J. Loize, *De Maillol et Codet à Sengalen: Les Amitiés du peintre Georges-Daniel de Monfreid et ses reliques de Gauguin,* (Paris, 1951), p. 31.) This is certainly too late. Maillol only used commercially dyed wool for his earliest tapestries after which he developed his own dyes.

34.   Even in 1937, Cladel says that the colors had faded drastically.

35.   Cladel, *Aristide Maillol*, p. 50.

36.   Paul Gauguin, "Exposition de la Libre Esthétique," *Essais d'art libre*, February-March 1894.

37.   Cladel, *Aristide Maillol*, p. 53.

38.   Maurice Denis, "Maillol et les Nabis," in *Aristide Maillol*, by Denis et al. (Paris: Cahiers Comoedia-Charpentier, November 1943).

39.   This tapestry is now in the Vierny collection.

40.   Morris had also faced this problem of light-sensitive chemical colors. (Howaldt, "Bildteppiche der Stilbewegung," p. 50.)

41.   Cladel, *Aristide Maillol*, p. 48.

42.   Ibid., p. 49.

43.   Ibid.

44.   Ibid.

45.   One drawing, showing one pair of women seated on a park bench, another pair set back a small distance in space and conversing, is in the Vierny collection. The other drawing was published in H.R. Hoetink, "Méditerranée meditaties," *Bulletin Museum Boymans van Beuningen*, no. 2 (1963). The oil sketch, *The Apple Pickers*, shows five women standing in a circle (Col. Samuel Josefowitz, Lausanne).

46.   Number 3 in Marcel Guerin, *Catalogue raisonné de l'oeuvre gravé et lithographié d'Aristide Maillol* (Geneva: P. Cailler, 1965).

47.   George Mauner, *The Nabis, Their History and Their Art: 1888-1896* (New York, Garland Publishing, Inc., 1978), p. 246.

48.   Tyson collection, Philadelphia Museum of Art.

49.   Gerald Needham, "Japanese Influence on French Painting," *Japonisme: Japanese Influence on French Art, 1854-1910* (Cleveland Museum of Art, Cleveland, Ohio, 1975), p. 124.

50.   Cladel, *Aristide Maillol*, p. 54. Both works are now located in the Danish Museum of Decorative Arts, Copenhagen.

51.   Van Marle, *Iconographie de l'Art Profane*, 1:101.

52. A.P. de Mirimonde, "La Musique dans les allégories de l'amour," *Gazette des Beaux-Arts,* ser. 6, 68 (November 1966): 265-90; and *Gazette des Beaux-Art* 69 (May-June 1967): 319-46.

53. In the Louvre.

54. Neither Blanc nor Müntz advance any hypotheses to explain the painting. Müntz states that it would be presumptuous to do so. Charles Blanc, *Histoire des Peintres: école Italienne,* vol. 8 (Paris: Jules Rénouard, 1868); E. Müntz, *Histoire de l'art pendant la Renaissance,* 3 vols. (Paris: Hachette, 1889-95).

55. Marcel Reymond, *"Le Concert Champêtre* de Giorgione," *Gazette des Beaux Arts,* ser. 4, 10 (November 1913): 433.

56. Mirimonde, "La Musique dans les allégories de l'amour," 68:277.

57. Ibid., p. 279.

58. John Rewald, "Maillol Remembered," preface of an exhibition catalogue, Solomon R. Guggenheim Museum, New York. *Aristide Maillol: 1861-1944* (1975-76), p. 11.

59. Favis, "The Garden of Love," pp. 142-43.

60. Octave Mirbeau, "Aristide Maillol," *La Revue des Revues* p. 324.

61. A detailed oil sketch for this tapestry exists in the Vierny Collection. The composition is virtually the same and a one-and-one-half inch border was left on all four sides.

62. Erik Lassen, "To Syede Billedtaepper af Maillol," *Kunstmuseets Arsskrift* (1944-45): 70.

63. Howaldt, "Bildteppiche der Stilbewegung," p. 53.

64. This painting is in the National Gallery of Art, London, acquired in 1861.

65. Georges Wildenstein, *Gauguin* (Paris: Les Beaux-Arts, 1964), no. 431.

66. Wildenstein, no. 430.

67. Wildenstein, no. 461, dated 1892. It was displayed at Gauguin's one-man show at Durand-Ruel in 1893.

68. This pose has been related to a figure of a classical Dionysius. Gauguin reused this figure in at least two later paintings: *Et l'Or de leur corps* (1901) (W. 596) and *Vairumati* (W. 559) and in at least three monotypes and a watercolor, *Auti Te Pape,* published by Rewald (fig. 65), and Hackelsberger, *Maillol—Méditerranée* (Stuttgart: Werkmonographien zur Bildenden Kunst, 1960).

69. Mauner provides a very complicated explanation of the symbolic significance of this device, using medieval numerology: three is the number of the Trinity, signifying all spiritual things, which with the addition of one, equals four, the number of all material things. It is unlikely that Maillol would have concerned himself with such abstruse thinking, but he might well have adapted the format without investigating its full meaning. Mauner, *The Nabis,* p. 238.

70. This work is now in the collection of the Bibesco family.

71. "Es gibt keinen französischen Bildteppich aus jener Epoche, auch keinen von Maillol selbst, wo einer vollkommenen dekorativen Form ein ähnlich mächtiger Inhalt verliehen worden ist." Howaldt, "Bildteppiche der Stilbewegung," p. 57-58.

72. Lassen, "To Syede Billedtaepper af Maillol," p. 65.

73. Perhaps this is the reason Hackelsberger dated the tapestry ca. 1896.

74. Howaldt, "Bildteppiche der Stilbewegung," p. 58.

75. Wendy Slatkin, "The Early Sculpture of Aristide Maillol, 1895-1900" La Gazette des Beaux-Arts, series 6, vol. 96 (October, 1980), p. 145.

76. Howaldt relates this also to a stone relief shown in the Salon de la Société Nationale des Beaux-Arts in 1903, where Maillol also pursues these stylistic principles in sculpture.

77. Cladel, Aristide Maillol, pp. 55-56.

78. In the collection of Dr. Gotthard Jedlicka, Zurich.

79. In the collection of the Museum of Modern Art, New York. For a recent discussion of a source for this work, see: Sidney Geist, "Maillol/Derré", Art Journal, XXXVI, no. 1 (1976), pp. 14-15.

80. Cladel, Aristide Maillol, p. 56.

Chapter 4

1. Maillol was enrolled in the sculpture section of the Ecole des Arts Décoratifs, when he was newly arrived in Paris in 1882-83. Unfortunately no works from his students days have survived.

2. Judith Cladel, Aristide Maillol: sa vie, son oeuvre et ses idées (Paris: Grasset, 1937), p. 57.

3. Ibid., p. 153; translated in John Rewald, Aristide Maillol (New York: Hyperion Press, 1939), p. 12.

4. Cladel, Aristide Maillol, p. 59.

5. Now in the collection of Bernheim Jeune Gallery.

6. Wendy Slatkin, "The Genesis of La Méditerranée," Art Journal 38 (Spring, 1979).

7. Quoted in René Puig, "La Vie misérable et glorieuse d'Aristide Maillol," Tramontane 49, nos 483-84, (1965), p. 18.

8. Cladel, Aristide Maillol, pp. 59-60.

9. Now in the collection of Mme. Vierny.

10. Both objects are in the collection of Mme. Vierny.

11. Cladel, Aristide Maillol, p. 58.

12. This work is located in SS. Giovanni and Paolo, Venice. It is illustrated in John Pope-Hennessey, An Introduction to Italian Sculpture, 2 vols. (London: Phaidon, 1955-63), fig. 162.

13. A rococo fountain of very similar shape was published as a line drawing in Albert Jacquemart, History of the Ceramic Art, trans. Bury Pallester (London: Low, 1873), with an inscription "Fait à Rennes, 1769-70."

14. Dr. Kathy Hiesinger, curator of Decorative Art at the Philadelpia Museum of Art, believes that it would have been more difficult to apply the designs and clay ornaments than to mold the whole form at one time. This would support my contention that Maillol was totally responsible for them.

15. Information supplied by Dr. Hiesinger.

16. One is reminded of the paintings *Two Nudes* and *Spring* in which Maillol uses the same figure in two different poses. The positioning of these three women also recalls a later sculptural grouping, *The Three Nymphs (Les Trois Nymphes)* (1937).

17. A drawing for this design is reproduced in Rewald, *Aristide Maillol,* p. 153.

18. In the collection of Dominique Denis, Marcel Guerin, *Catalogue raisonné de l'oeuvre gravé et lithographié d'Aristide Maillol* (Geneva: P. Cailler, 1965, no. 263.

19. Octave Mirbeau, *Aristide Maillol* (Paris: Société des Dilettantes, 1921), p. 99.

20. There are, naturally, exceptions to this general rule. For example, the three paintings in the Petit Palais depict nude women (figs. 14, 15, 17). A group of early bronze statuettes are clothed as are three large-scale figures, dressed in simple, form-revealing drapery: *La Douleur,* the *Monument to the Dead of Port-Vendres* and the *Flora.*

21. Maurice Denis, "Définition du néo-traditionnalisme," *Théories 1890-1910: Du Symbolism et du Gauguin vers un nouvel ordre classique* (3rd ed., Paris: Bibliotèque de l'Occident, 1913), p. 6.

22. Mark Roskill, *Van Gogh, Gauguin, and the Impressionist Circle* (Greenwich, Conn.: New York Graphic Society, 1970), p. 93.

23. According to Rewald, this life sized statue is a direct enlargement of a statuette created in 1898.

24.. André Gide, "Promenade au Salon d'Automne," *Gazette des Beaux Arts,* ser. 3, 34 (December 1905): 476.

25. Cladel, *Aristide Maillol,* p. 58.

26. Georges Besson, "De Rodin à Maillol," *Le Point* (December 1937), p. 241.

27. Jean Cassou, introduction to *Hommage à Maillol,* exhibition catalogue, Musée National d'Art Moderne, Paris, 1961, n.p.

28. Cladel, *Aristide Maillol,* pp. 129, 132.

29. Possibly the figures reproduced in Rewald, *Aristide Maillol,* pp. 121 or 126.

30. René Puig, "La Vie misérable et glorieuse d'Aristide Maillol," *Tramontane* 49, nos. 483-84, p. 21.

31. Waldemar-George, *Maillol* (Paris: Arted, Editions d'Art, 1971), p. 74.

32. Patrick McCaughey, "The Monolith and Modernist Sculpture," *Art International,* no. 9 (1970).

33. Maillol, quoted in Waldemar-George, *Aristide Maillol* (Greenwich, Conn. New York Graphic Society, 1965), p. 39.

34. The Petit Palais, which has a number of the original terracottas, dates them 1896. Stylistically they belong with paintings and tapestries executed around that time, and clearly predate works executed ca. 1900. (This will be discussed shortly in the text.) Monfreid's journal records many occasions during that year and 1897 when Maillol baked his sculptures in his oven. This evidence, taken together seems to strongly suggest 1896 as the most probable date for their execution.

35. Mirbeau, "Aristide Maillol," pp. 333-34.

36. Slatkin, "The Genesis of *La Mediterranée.,*" p. 188.

37.   Cladel, *Aristide Maillol*, p. 132.

38.   Mirbeau, "Aristide Maillol," p. 323.

39.   G.M. Butcher, "Reflections on Maillol," *The Arts Review* 34, no. 17 (September 1961): 20.

40.   Hoetink dates it 1893, but that seems to be too early. *The Spring* could not have been sculpted before 1896, and is close, stylistically, to *The Washerwoman.*

41.   The position of the figure in this drawing very closely resembles the figure on the right, in the painting of the same title, seen from a different angle (Fig. 18).

42.   Both drawings are in the Collection Dina Vierny, Paris.

43.   Waldemar-George, *Aristide Maillol*, pp. 47-48.

Conclusion

1.   See Slatkin, "The Early Sculpture of Maillol: 1895-1900," *La Gazette des Beaux-Arts,* series 6, vol. 96 (October, 1980).

Epilogue

1.   Maillol did evolve a variety of original poses for the *Monument to the Dead* at Banyuls, but this was in response to a specific site and relief format, and is not characteristic of the oeuvre.

2.   Berthold Hackelsberger, *Maillol—Méditerranée* (Stuttgart: Philipp Reclam, 1960).

3.   This watercolor is reproduced in Hackelsberger, *Maillol—Méditerranée,* p. 16. Gauguin's image originated in a painting of the same title (W. 538) of 1892.

4.   For a complete discussion of the development of *The Mediterranean,* see Wendy Slatkin, "The Genesis of *La Méditerranée,*" *Art Journal* 38 (Spring 1979).

5.   This date is established in John Rewald, *Aristide Maillol* (New York: Hyperion Press, 1939).

6.   Ibid., illustrated, pp. 74-75.

7.   John Rewald, "Une Nouvelle oeuvre de Maillol—*l'Air,*" *Beaux-Arts,* no. 318 (February 3, 1939), n.p.

8.   Judith Cladel, *Aristide Maillol; Sa Vie, son oeuvre et ses idées* (Paris: Grasset, 1937), p. 147.

9.   René Puig, "La Vie misérable et glorieuse d'Aristide Maillol," *Tramontane* 49, nos. 483-84 (1965), p. 30.

10.   Cladel, *Aristide Maillol*, p. 127.

11.   Ibid.

12.   Ibid., p. 132.

13.   Henri Frère, *Conversations avec Maillol* (Geneva: P. Cailler, 1950), p. 273.

14.   Denis, "Aristide Maillol," in *Théories,* (Paris, Bibliotèque de l'Occident, 1913), p. 228.

15.   Stump, "Maillol in the 1890's," The Register of the Museum of Art, University of Kansas 4 (March 1971), p. 43. The same idea is in Waldemar-George, *Aristide Maillol,* (Greenwich, Conn. New York Graphic Society, 1965), pp. 47-48.

16.   Alfred Kuhn, *Maillol* (Landschaft, Werke, Gesprüche, Leipzig, 1925), p. 13.

17. Cladel, *Aristide Maillol*, p. 148.

18. Maurice Denis, preface to catalogue of exhibition, Galerie Parvillé, Paris, *L'Ecole de Pont-Aven et les Nabis: 1888-9* (1943).

19. Sérusier, quoted in Charles Chassé, *The Nabis and their Period* (New York: Praeger, 1969), p. 56.

20. From the introduction by Maurice Denis to Paul Sérusier, *A, B, C de la Peinture* (Paris: 1943), p. 64.

21. Robert Rosenblum, *Modern Painting and the Northern Romantic Tradition: Friedrich to Rothko* (New York: 1975), p. 103.

22. Cladel, *Aristide Maillol*, p. 146.

23. Rewald, "Maillol Remembered," p. 12.

24. *The Mediterranean* has been discussed extensively in: Hackelsberger, *Maillol—Méditerranée;* H.R. Hoetink, "Méditerranée meditatiés," *Bulletin Museum Boymans van Beuningen* (Rotterdam: 1963), pp. 30-55; and Slatkin, "The Genesis of *La Méditerranéne.*"

25. Hamilton, *Painting and Sculpture in Europe: 1880-1940*, (Baltimore, Penguin Books, 1967), pp. 95-96.

26. Reproduced in Rewald, *Aristide Maillol*, p. 34.

27. Marcel Duchamp, "The Creative Act," reprinted in the *New Art*, ed. Gregory Battock (New York: E.P. Dutton, 1966).

Appendix

1. For an extensive technical analysis see: Gabriele Howaldt, "Bildteppich der Stilbewegung," *Kunst in Hessen und am Mittelrhein: Schriften der Hessischen Museen* (Darmstadt, no. 4, 1964); and Erik Lassen, "To Syede Billedtaepper af Maillol," *Kunstmuseets Arsskrift* (Copenhagen, 1944-45).

2. Howaldt, "Bildteppich der Stilbewegung," p. 53.

3. Illustrated in Rewald, *Aristide Maillol*, illustration no. 9, listed as property of Galerie Bernheim-Jeune.

4. Now in the Collection Vierny. Illustrated in R. Barilli, *Il Simbolismo nella Pittura Francese dell-Ottocento* (Milan: Fratelli Fabri Editori, 1967), Plate XLV.

Bibliography

Acts of the Twentieth International Congress of the History of Art. *Studies in Western Art: Problems of the Nineteenth and Twentieth Centuries*, vol. 4. Princeton: Princeton University Press, 1963.

Alazard, Jean. "Aristide Maillol." *Dedalo*, vol. 8 (1927-28).

Andersen, Wayne. *Gauguin's Paradise Lost*. New York: Viking Press, 1971.

Aurier, Albert. "Deuxième exposition des peintres impressionnistes et symbolistes." *Mercure de France* 2 (March 1891): 155-65.

_____. "Les Peintres symbolistes." *La Revue encyclopédique* April, 1892).

_____. *Oeuvres Posthumes*. Paris, 1893.

Bacou, Rosalinde. "Décors d'appartements au temps des Nabis." *Art de France* 4 (March 1964): 190-205.

Barazetti-Desmoulins, Suzanne. *Maurice Denis, 25 Novembre 1870, 13 Novembre 1943*. Preface by Robert Rey. Paris: Grasset, 1945.

Barilli, R. *Il Simbolismo nella pittura francese dell' Ottocento*. Milan: Fratelli Fabri, Editori, 1967.

Battock, Gregory, ed. *The New Art*. New York: E.P. Dutton, 1966.

Bazin, G., and Chassé, C. "Les Nabis et le groupe Bonnard, Vuillard, Roussel." *L'Amour de l'art*, no. 4 (April 1933).

Besson, Georges. "De rodin à Maillol." *Le Point*, December 1937.

Blanc, Charles. *Grammaire des arts décoratifs*. Paris, 1882.

_____. *Grammaire des arts du dessin*. Paris, 1867.

_____. *Histoire des Peintres*. Vol. 8: *Ecole Italienne*. Paris: Jules Renouard, 1868.

Bodelsen, Merete. *Gauguin's Ceramics: A Study in the Development of His Art*. London: Faber and Faber, 1964.

_____. "The Missing Link in Gauguin's Cloisonism." *Gazette des Beaux Arts*, ser. 6, 53 (May-June 1959): 329-44.

Boime, Albert. *The Academy and French Painting in the Nineteenth Century*. London: Phaidon, 1971.

Bonnard, P.; P. Camo; A. Maillol; L. Masse; J.S. Pons; and A. Suspluges, "Aristide Maillol." *Cahiers des amis de l'art*, no. 10, 1946.

Bouvier, Marguette. *Aristide Maillol*. Lausanne; Editions Marguerat, 1945.

Brassai. "J'ai vu vivre Maillol." *Lectures Pour Tous*, August 1961.

Brillant, M. *Portrait de Maurice Denis*. Paris: Bloud & Gay, 1945.

Busch, Gunter. *Aristide Maillol als Illustrator*. Neu-Isenburg: W. Tiessen, 1970.

Butcher, G.M. "Reflections on Maillol." *The Arts Review* 13 (September 1961): 20.

Cailler, Pierre. *Catalogue raisonné de l'oeuvre gravé et lithographié de Maurice Denis*. Geneva: P. Cailler, 1968.

Camo, Pierre. *Maillol, mon ami: sa vie, son amitié, son art*. Lausanne: Editions du Grand-Chêne, 1950.

Cann, Louise G. "The Engraved Work of Maillol." *The Arts* 14 (October 1928): 200-203.

Cassou, Jean. "*La Rivière* d'Aristide Maillol." *Musées de France* (July 1948), pp. 137-38.

Charbonneux, Jean. *Maillol.* Paris: Braun, 1947.

Chassé, Charles. "Gauguin et Mallarmé." *L'Amour de l'art,* August 1922.

————. *Gauguin et son temps.* Paris: Bibliotèque des arts, 1950.

————. *Le Mouvement symboliste dans l'art du XIXe siècle.* Paris: Librairie Floury, 1947.

————. *The Nabis and Their Period.* Translated by Michael Bullock. New York: Praeger, 1969.

————. "Les Nabis et l'imitation des maîtres." *L'Amour de l'art* (1933), pp. 69-82.

————. "Paul Sérusier." *L'Art et les artistes* 15 (May 1927): 260-67.

————. *D'Ubu Roi au Douanier Rousseau.* Paris. Nouvelle Revue Critique, 1947.

Chermet, Raymond. "Maillol rapelle le principe des arts plastiques." *Arts,* vol. 16 (June 28-July 4, 1961).

Chevalier, Denys. *Maillol.* Paris: Flammarion, 1970.

Chipp, Herschel B. *Theories of Modern Art: A Source Book by Artists and Critics.* Berkeley: University of California Press, 1968.

Cladel, Judith. *Aristide Maillol: sa vie, son oeuvre et ses idées.* Paris: Grasset, 1937.

————. "Maillol devant le modèle." *Verve,* vol. 1 (December 1937).

Cogniat, Raymond. "Aristide Maillol." *L'Art vivant,* 1937, p. 117.

Crary, J. "Idealism of Maillol". *ARTS Magazine* 50 (January 1976): 70-71.

Denis, Maurice. "Aristide Maillol." *Occident,* November 1905. Republished by G. Crès; Collection de Cahiers d'aujourd'hui, Paris, 1925. Also reprinted in *Théories.* Paris: Bibliotèque de l'Occident, 1913.

————. *Du Symbolism au classicism: Théories.* Edited by O. Revault d'Allones. Paris: Hermann, Miroirs de l'art, 1964.

————. *Journal.* 3 vols. Paris: La Colombe, 1957-59.

————. *Théories 1890-1910: Du Symbolism et de Gauguin vers un nouvel ordre classique.* 3d ed. Paris: Bibliotèque de l'occident, 1913.

Denis, Maurice; P. Valery; A. Perret; P. du Columbier; and C. Roy, *Aristide Maillol.* Paris: Cahiers Comoedia-Charpentier, November 1943.

Dorival, Bernard. *Les Etapes de la peinture française.* 3 vols. Paris: Gallimard, 1946.

————. "Musée d'Art Moderne: Nabis et Cubistes." *Bulletin des Musées de France* (May-June 1947), pp. 9-22.

Dormoy, Marie. "Maillol Illustrateur." *Arts et métiers graphiques,* no. 55 (1936), pp. 37-41.

Dreyfus, Albert. "Aristide Maillol." *Deutsche Kunst und Dekoration* (1926-27), pp. 303-5.

————. "Der Bildhauer Maillol." *Deutsche Kunst und Dekoration* (April 1932), pp. 23-24.

Dujardin, Edward. "Aux XX et aux Indépendants—le Cloisonisme." *Revue indépendant,* March 1888.

Dupont, J. "Les Nabis: Maurice Denis et les décorateurs." *L'Amour de l'art* (April 1933), pp. 73-78.

Eckstein, Hans. "Aristide Maillol zu seinem 75 Geburtstag." *Kunst für Alle,* January 1937.

Elsen, Albert. *Origins of Modern Sculpture.* New York: G. Braziller, 1974.

Fagus, Félicien. "Durio, Bocquet, Maillol." *La Revue blanche* 27 (January 1902): 65.

————. "Maillol." *La Revue blanche* 28 (August 1902): 550-51.

Favis, Roberta S. "The Garden of Love in Fifteenth Century Netherlandish and German Engravings: Some studies in secular iconography in the late Middle Ages and early Renaissance." Ph.D. dissertation, University of Pennsylvania, 1974.

Fehl, Philip. "The Hidden Genre: A Study of the *Concert Champêtre* in the Louvre." *Journal of Aesthetics and Art Criticism,* vol. 16 (December 1957).

Fénéon, Félix. "Exposition du groupe impressionniste et synthétiste, Café Volpini." *La Cravache,* July 6, 1889.

————. "La VIIIe exposition impressionniste." Reprinted in *Au-delà de l'impressionnisme.* Edited by Françoise Cachin. Paris: Hermann, Miroirs de l'art, 1966.

Fierens, Paul, and Sentenac, P. "Maillol." *L'Art et les artistes,* vols. 27-28 (1933-34).

Fontainas, André. "L'Oeuvre récente d'Aristide Maillol." *Formes,* no. 19 (November 1931), pp. 148-50.

_____. *Mes souvenirs du symbolisme.* Paris: La Nouvelle Revue Critique, 1928.

de Forges, Marie-Thérèse. "Un Nouvelle tableau de Puvis de Chavannes au Musée du Louvre." *La Revue du Louvre et des musées de France* 20 (1970): 248-52.

Frère, Henri. *Conversations avec Maillol.* Geneva: P. Cailler, 1950.

Fry, Roger. "Aristide Maillol." *Burlington Magazine* 17 (1910): 26-32.

Ganz, Hermann. "Maillol, Cézanne—Denkmal." *Kunst und Kunstler* (1929-30), pp. 211-12.

Gasquet, J. "Aristide Maillol." *Le Feu,* May 1912.

Gauguin, Paul. "Exposition de la Libre Esthétique." *Essais d'art libre,* February-March 1894.

_____. *Lettres à Georges-Daniel de Monfreid.* Preface by Victor Segalen, Paris, 1926.

Gauss, Charles E. *The Aesthetic Theories of French Artists.* Baltimore: Johns Hopkins University Press, 1949.

Gautier, E.P. "Lithographs of the Revue Blanche: 1893-95." *Magazine of Art* 45 (October 1952): 273-78.

Geffroy, Gustave. *La Vie artistique.* Paris, 1892-1903.

Geist, Sidney. "Maillol/Derre." *Art Journal* XXXVI, no. 1 (1976): 14-15.

Gervais, André Charles. *Marionettes et marionnettistes de France.* Paris, 1947.

Gide, André. "Promenade au Salon d'Automne." *Gazette des Beaux-Arts,* ser. 3, 34 (December 1905): 475-86.

_____. *Si le Grain ne Meurt.* Paris: Gallimard, 1931.

Giedion-Welcker, Carola. *Modern Plastic Art.* Zürich: Girsberger, 1937.

Giono, Jean. "*Les Géorgiques* de Virgile illustrés par le sculpteur Maillol et imprimés par Gonin." *Minotaure,* nos. 12-13 (May 1939).

Girou, Jean. *Sculpteurs du midi.* Paris, 1938.

Göbel, Heinrich. *Tapestries of the Lowlands.* Translated by Robert West. New York: Hacker Art Books, 1924.

Godwin, B.M. "A Maillol Masterpiece." *Art News of the Toledo Museum,* no. 76 (September 1936).

Goldwater, Robert. "Puvis de Chavannes: Some Reasons for a Reputation." *Art Bulletin* 28 (1946): 33-43.

_____. "Symbolist Art and Theater." *Magazine of Art* 39 (December 1946): 366-70.

Gordon, Donald. *Modern Art Exhibitions: 1900-1916.* 2 vols. Munich: Prestel-Verlag, 1974.

Gottlieb, A. "Aristide Maillol." *Deutsche Kunst und Dekoration* (January 1931), pp. 259-60.

Gradman, Erwin. "Maillol als Zeichner." *Graphis* 1 (1945): 107-13.

Grand-Chastel, P.M., and Coulonges, Henri. *Maillol.* Paris: Hachette, Chefs-d'oeuvres de l'art, 1969.

Gray, Basil. *Persian Painting.* London: Collins, 1961.

Gray, Christopher. *Sculpture and Ceramics of Paul Gauguin.* Baltimore: Johns Hopkins Press, 1963.

Grohman, Willi. "Enquète sur la sculpture en Allemagne et en France." *Cahiers d'Art,* 1928.

Gruyer, Gustave. "Vittore Pisano." *Gazette des Beaux-Arts,* 3d period, 10 (November 1893): 353-68.

Guenne, Jacques. "La Grandeur d'Aristide Maillol." *Art Vivant,* May 1933.

Guerin, Marcel. *Catalogue raisonné de l'oeuvre gravé et lithographié d'Aristide Maillol.* Geneva: P. Cailler, 1965.

Guiffrey, Jean, gen. ed. *La Peinture au Musée du Louvre.* Paris: L'Illustration, 1929. Vol. 2: *Ecole italienne primitifs,* by Louis Hautecoeur.

Guiffrey, Jules. *Histoire de la tapisserie depuis le Moyen Age jusqu'a nos jours.* Tours: Alfred Mame et fils, 1886.

Guiffrey, J.M.J.; E. Müntz, ; and A. Pinchart, *Histoire de la tapisserie en France.* 2 vols. Paris: Société anonyme des publications périodiques, 1878-85.

Guillemet, Maurice. "Aristide Maillol." *Les Carnets des Artistes,* September 15, 1917.

Guy, Cécile. "Le Barc de Boutteville." *L'Oeil,* no. 124 (1965), pp. 31-38.

Hackelsberger, Berthold. *Maillol—Méditerranée.* Werkmonographien zur Bildenden Kunst, no. 56. Stuttgart: Philipp Reclam, 1960.

Hamilton, G.H. *Painting and Sculpture in Europe: 1880-1940.* Baltimore: Penguin Books, 1967.

Harlor, Mme. "Maillol." *La Fronde,* June 26, 1902.

Harrison, Martin, and Waters, Bill. *Burne-Jones.* London: Putnam, 1973.

Haug, Hans. *La Peinture française au Musée des Beaux-Arts de Strasbourg.* Strasbourg, 1955.

Hautecoeur, Louis. *Emile Bernard.* Paris, 1962.

Hentzen, Alfred. "Buchillustrationen von Maillol." *Philobiblon* 7 (1938): 336-46.

Herban, Mathew. "Maurice Denis' 'Nouvel Ordre Classique' as contained in his *Théories.*" Ph.D. dissertation, University of Pennsylvania, 1972.

Herbert, R. "City vs. Country: The Rural Image in French Painting from Millet to Gauguin." *Artforum* 8 (February 1970): 44-55.

Hermann, Fritz. *Die Revue Blanche und die Nabis.* 2 vols. Munich, 1959. Microcopy.

Hildebrand, Adolf von. *Das Problem der Form in der Bildenden Kunst.* Strasbourg: Heitz and Mündel, 1903.

Hobhouse, Janet. "Reverence and Eroticism". *Art News* 75, no. 3 (March, 1976): 36-38.

Hoetink, H.R. "Méditerranée meditaties." *Bulletin Museum Boymans van Beuningen,* Rotterdam, no. 2 (1963).

Howaldt, Gabriele. "Bildteppiche der Stilbewegung." *Kunst in Hessen und am Mittelrhein: Schriften der Hessischen Museen,* Darmstadt, no. 4 (1964).

Humbert, Agnès. *Les Nabis et leur époque.* Geneva: P. Cailler, 1954.

Huret, T.H. "Le Banquet des Symbolistes." *Echo de Paris,* February 4, 1891.

Huysmans, J.K. *Certains: G. Moreau, Degas, Cheret, Whistler, Rops.* Paris, 1889.

Jacquemart, Albert. *A History of the Ceramic Art.* Translated by Bury Pallester. London: Low, 1873.

Jaworska, Wladyslawa. *Gauguin and the Pont Aven School.* Translated by Patrick Evans. Greenwich, Conn.: New York Graphic Society, 1972.

Jianou, Ionel, and Dufet, Michel. *Bourdelle.* Paris: Editions d'art, 1965.

Jobe, Joseph. *Le Grand livre de la tapisserie.* Lausanne, 1965.

Jullian, Philippe. "Autour de trois peintres symbolistes, d'étranges beautés." *Plaisir de France,* June 1971.

———. *Dreamers of Decadence: Symbolist Painters of the 1890's.* Translated by Robert Baldick. New York: Praeger, 1971.

———. *The Symbolists.* Translated by Mary Anne Stevens. New York: Praeger, 1973.

———. *The Triumph of Art Nouveau: The Paris Exhibition, 1900.* London: Phaidon, 1974.

Kahn, Gustave. "L'Art français à l'exposition." *La Vogue,* vol. 2 (August 1889).

Kessler, Harry. *Maillol.* Translated by J.H. Mason. London, 1930.

———. *Souvenirs d'un Européen.* Translated by Blaise Briod. Paris, 1936.

Kuhn, Alfred. *Maillol: landschaft, werke, gespräche.* Leipzig, 1925.

Kuhnen, Sigrid. "Aristide Maillol: Das druckgraphische Werk." Ph.D. dissertation, University of Vienna, 1973.

Lafargue, Marc; Octave Mirbeau; Pierre Camo; and Jean Girou. *Aspects de Maillol.* Albi: Editions du Languedoc, 1945.

Lassen, Erik. "To Syede Billedtaepper af Maillol." *Kunstmuseets Arsskrift,* Copenhagen (1944-45), pp. 65-75.

Lehmann, A.G. *The Symbolist Aesthetic in France: 1885-95.* Oxford: Blackwell, 1950.

Lethève, Jacques. "La Connaissance des Pré-Raphaélites anglaises en France: 1885-1900." *Gazette des Beaux-Arts,* ser. 6, 53 (May-June 1959): 363-74.

_____. *Impressionists et Symbolistes devant la presse.* Paris: Max Le Clerc et Cie., Librairie Armand Colin, 1959.

_____. "Les Salons de la Rose + Croix." *Gazette des Beaux-Arts,* ser. 6, 56 (December 1960): 363-74.

Levinson, A. "Sculpteurs de ce temps." *L'Amour de l'art,* November 1924.

Levy, Mervyn. *Drawings and Sculpture.* Bath: Somerset, 1970.

Licht, Fred. *Sculpture: Nineteenth and Twentieth Centuries.* Greenwich, Conn.: New York Graphic Society, 1967.

Linnenkamp, Rolf. *Aristide Maillol—Die Grossen Plastiken.* Munich: F. Bruckman, 1960.

Loize, J. *De Maillol et Codet à Ségalen: Les Amitiés du peintre Georges-Daniel de Monfreid et ses reliques de Gauguin.* Paris, 1951.

Lövgren, Sven. *The Genesis of Modernism: Seurat, Gauguin, Van Gogh and French Symbolism in the 1880s.* Stockholm: Almquist & Wiksell, 1959.

Lugné-Pöe. *Le Sot du Tremplin.* Vol. 1: *Souvenirs et impressions du théâtre.* Paris: Gallimard, Editions de la nouvelle revue Française, 1931.

Lyons, Lisa. "Aristide Maillol: Monument to Debussy". *Toledo Art Museum News* XVII, no. 3 (1974): 62-64.

McCaughey, Patrick. "The Monolith and Modernist Sculpture." *Art International* 14 (September 1970): 19-24.

Malingue, Maurice. "Petites et grands Nabis." *L'Oeil,* no. 62 (February 1960), pp. 36-45.

Marussi, G. "Odilon Redon et les Nabis." *Le Arti,* November 1963.

Mauner, George. *The Nabis, Their History and Their Art: 1888-1896.* New York and London, Garland Publishing, Inc., 1978 (Ph.D. dissertation, Columbia University, 1966).

_____. "The Nature of Nabi Symbolism." *Art Journal* 23 (1964): 96-103.

Mellerio, A. *Le Mouvement idéaliste en peinture.* Paris, 1896.

Mirbeau, Octave. "Aristide Maillol." *La Revue des Revues,* April 1905. Reprinted in monograph. Paris: Sociéte des Dilettantes, 1921.

Mirimonde, A.P. de. *L'Iconographie Musicale sous les Rois Bourbons: La Musique dans les Arts Plastiques, XVIIe—XVIIIe siècles.* Paris, 1975.

_____. "La Musique dans les allégories de l'amour." *Gazette des Beaux-Arts,* ser. 6, 68 (November 1966): 265-90, and 69 (May-June 1967): 319-46.

Morice, Charles. "Le Salon d'Automne." *Mercure de France* 58 (December 1905): 376-93.

Morris, William. *Textiles—Part I.* Introductory notes to the catalogue of the first exhibition of the Arts and Crafts Society. London, 1888.

Müntz, E. *Histoire de l'art pendant la Renaissance.* 3 vols. Paris: Hachette, 1889-95.

_____. *La Tapisserie.* Paris: Bibliotèque de l'enseignement des Beaux-Arts, 1882.

Natanson, Thadée. "Des Peintres intelligents." *La Revue blanche* 22 (May 1900): 53-56.

_____. "Neuvième exposition de la Société des Artistes Indépendants." *La Revue blanche* 4 (April 1893) 271-76.

_____. "Sur une exposition des peintres de *La Revue blanche.*" *Arts et Métiers graphiques.* No. 54 (August 1936): 9-18.

_____. "Une date de l'histoire de la peinture Française: Mars, 1899." *La Revue blanche* 18 (April 1899): 504-12.

Naylor, Gillian. *The Arts and Crafts Movement.* Cambridge: MIT Press, 1971.

Negri, Renata. *Bonnard e i Nabis.* Milan: Fratelli Fabri Editori, 1967.

d'Ors, Eugenio, and Lassaigne, Jacques. *Almanach des Arts.* Paris: Fayard, 1938.

Paccagnini, Giovanni. *Pisanello.* Translated by June Carroll. New York: Phaidon, 1973.

Petrotchouk, O. *Maillol.* Moscow: Edition Art, 1977.

Pilon, Edmond. "Beaux arts peintures impressionnistes et symbolistes." *La Plume,* March 15, 1894.

Pimienta, Gustave. "Aristide Maillol." *Le Point,* 1937.

Pincus-Witten, R. "The Iconography of Symbolist Painting." *Artforum* 8 (January 1970): 56-62.

————. "Ideal Interlude: The First Retrospective of the Salons de la Rose + Croix." *Artforum* 7 (September 1968): 51-55.

Piroli, Thomas, engraver. *Les Monuments antiques du Musée Napoléon.* Commentary by Louis Petit Radel. 2 vols. Paris: F. et P. Piranesi, Frères, 1804.

La Plume. "Aux peintres novateurs indépendants." No. 57 (September 1, 1891), entire issue.

Pope-Hennessey, John. *An Introduction to Italian Sculpture.* London: Phaidon, 1955-58.

Puig, René. "La Vie misérable et glorieuse d'Aristide Maillol." *Tramontane* 49, nos. 483-84 (1965): 1-52.

Reff, Theodore. "Cézanne and Poussin." *Journal of the Warburg and Courtauld Institutes* 23 (January 1960) 150-74.

René-Jean. "Aristide Maillol à Marly." *Beaux-Arts,* no. 39 (September 29, 1933).

Rewald, John. *Aristide Maillol.* New York, Paris, London: Hyperion Press, 1939.

————. "Aristide Maillol." *Marianne,* January 1938.

————. "Les Ateliers de Maillol." *Le Point,* no. 17 (1938).

————. "For Aristide Maillol on his 80th Birthday." *Art News* 40 (December 1941): 19ff.

————. *The History of Impressionism.* 4th ed. New York: Museum of Modern Art, 1973.

————. "Last Visit with Maillol." *Magazine of Art* 38 (May 1945): 154-57.

————. "Maillol Illustrateur." *Le Portique,* vol. 1 (1945).

————. *Paul Gauguin.* New York, London, Paris: Hyperion Press, 1938.

————. *Post-Impressionism: From Van Gogh to Gauguin.* 2d ed. New York: Museum of Modern Art, 1962.

————. "Reflexions autour de la *Pomone* d'Aristide Maillol." *La Renaissance,* March 1935.

————. "Une Nouvelle oeuvre de Maillol—*l'Air.*" *Beaux-Arts,* no. 318 (February 3, 1939).

————. *The Woodcuts of Aristide Maillol: A Complete Catalogue.* New York: Pantheon Books, 1943.

————, ed. *Camille Pisarro: Letters to His Son Lucien.* Translated by Lionel Abel. New York: Pantheon Books, 1943.

Rey, Robert. "Aristide Maillol et la ville de Paris." *Cahiers d'Art* 3 (1928): 360.

————. *La Renaissance du sentiment classique.* Paris, 1921.

Reymond, Marcel. "*Le Concert Champêtre* de Giorgione." *Gazette des Beaux-Arts,* ser. 4, 10 (November 1913): 431-36.

Rippl-Ronai. Paris, 1944, with an introduction by François Gachat.

Roger-Marx, Claude. "Aristide Maillol à L'Acropole." *Formes et Couleurs* 5 (1943): 2-11.

————. *French Original Engravings from Manet to the Present Time.* London, Paris, New York: Hyperion Press, 1939.

Romains, Jules. *Maillol.* Paris: Flammarion, 1948.

————. "Maillol." *Formes,* no. 4 (1930).

Ronnebeck, A. "Maillol Speaks." *The Arts,* 1924.

————. "The Teachings of Maillol from a Paris Diary." *The Arts,* 1924.

Rookmaaker, H.R. *Synthetist Art Theories—Genesis and Nature of the Ideas on Art of Gauguin and his circle.* Amsterdam: Swets and Zeitlinger, 1959.

Rosenblum, Robert. *Modern Painting and the Northern Romantic Tradition: Friedrich to Rothko.* New York, 1975.

Roskill, Mark. "Early Impressionism and the Fashion Print." *Burlington Magazine* 112 (June 1970): 391-95.

————. *Van Gogh, Gauguin and the Impressionist Circle.* Greenwich, Conn.: New York Graphic Society, 1970.

Salomon, Jacques. *Vuillard.* Forward by John Rewald. Paris: Gallimard, 1968.

Scheffler, Karl. "Aristide Maillol." *Kunst und Kunstler,* January 1929.

Schmutzler, Robert. *Art Nouveau.* Translated by Edouard Roditi. New York: H.N. Abrams, 1964.

Schopenhauer, Arthur. *The World as Will and Representation.* 2 vols. Translated by E.F.J. Payne. New York: Dover Press, 1966. Reprint of the Falcon's Wing Press, Indian Hills, Colorado, 1958.

Schubert, D. "Anmerkungen zur Kunst Lehmbrucks" *Pantheon* 39 (January-March, 1981): 59-60.

Selvig, Forrest. "Les Nabis, Prophets of the Vanguard." *Art News* 61 (1962): 34-37 and 64-68.

Selz, Peter. *Art Nouveau—Art and Design at the Turn of the Century.* New York: Museum of Modern Art, 1959.

Sentenac, Paul. "La Vie aux heures claires d'Aristide Maillol." *L'Art et les Artistes,* vol. 28 (1933-34).

Sérusier, Paul. *A B C de la Peinture.* Paris, 1943. Introduction by Maurice Denis: "Sérusier, sa vie, son oeuvre."

Shattuck, Roger. *The Banquet Years.* New York: Harcourt Brace, 1955.

Sharp Young, Mahonri. "Maillol Remembered." *Apollo,* CIII, no. 171 (May, 1976): 438-39.

Slatkin, Wendy. "The Early Sculpture of Maillol: 1895-1900". *La Gazette des Beaux-Arts,* series 6, vol. 96 (October 1980): 141-48.

_____. "The Genesis of Maillol's *La Méditerranée".* *Art Journal* 38 (Spring 1979): 184-89.

_____. "Reminiscences of Maillol: A Conversation with Dina Vierny." *ARTS Magazine* 54 (September 1979): 164-67.

Stratem, Jean, and Stratem, Donald. "The Nabis and Their Circle." *Minneapolis Institute of Arts Bulletin* 51 (1962): 121-52.

Stump, Jeanne. "Maillol in the 1890's." *Register of the Museum of Art, University of Kansas* 4 (March 1971): 34-47.

Sutter, Jean. *The Neo-Impressionists.* Greenwich, Conn.: New York Graphic Society, 1970.

Svensson, George. "Maillol som bokillustrator." *Biblis* (1968), pp. 9-60.

Thierry, Norbert. "A propos de Maillol." *France,* March 7, 1947.

Thirion, Yvonne. "L'influence de l'estampe japonaise dans l'oeuvre de Gauguin." *Gazette des Beaux-Arts,* ser. 6, 47 (January-April 1956): 95-114.

_____. "De l'Influence de l'estampe japonaise sur la peinture française dans le seconde moitié du XIXe siècle." Master's thesis, Paris.

Vachon, Marius. *Puvis de Chavannes.* Paris: Braun, 1895.

Valentiner, W.R. "*Bust of Venus* by Aristide Maillol." *Bulletin of the Detroit Institute of Arts,* 1929-30.

Vallance, Aymer. "The Revival of Tapestry-weaving: An interview with Mr. William Morris." *Studio,* vol. 3 (July 1894).

Van Marle, Raimond. *Iconographie de l'art profane.* 2 vol. The Hague: M. Nijhoff, 1931-32.

Verkade, Jan. *Le Tourment de Dieu.* Paris, 1923.

Vierny, Dina. "Autour de Maillol." *Art et Industrie,* vols. 17-18 (December 1950).

Vincent, Cécile. "Maurice Denis et Maillol." *Information de l'histoire de l'art* 15 (1970): 209-15.

Vollard, Ambrose. *Recollections of a Picture Dealer.* Translated by Violet M. McDonald. Boston: Little, Brown & Co., 1936.

Waldemar-George. *Aristide Maillol.* Translated by Diana Imber. Greenwich, Conn.: New York Graphic Society, 1965.

_____. "Aristide Maillol." *The Arts* 5 (February 1924): 84-169.

_____. *Aristide Maillol et l'âme de la sculpture.* Neuchâtel: Editions Ides et Calendes, 1964, 2nd ed., 1977.

_____. *Maillol.* Paris: Arted, Editions d'Art, 1971.

_____. "Maillol ou le miracle français." *Arts et Décoration,* January 1936.

Waldvogel, M. "The Nabis and Their Circle: 1890-1900." *Art International* 7 (January 1963): 55-58.

Wallis, A. Armstrong. "The Symbolist Painters of 1890." *Marsyas* 1 (1941): 117-52.
Wildenstein, Georges. *Gauguin.* Paris: Les Beaux-Arts, 1964.
Wooster, Ann-Sargent. Review of exhibition at the Guggenheim Museum, New York, 1975-76. *Artforum* 14 (March, 1976) 66.

Exhibitions

Durand Ruel Gallery, Paris. *Puvis de Chavannes* (1887). Preface by R. Ballu.
Galerie du Barc de Boutteville, Paris. *Onzième exposition des peintres impressionistes et symbolistes* (1896).
Galerie A. Vollard, Paris. *Aristide Maillol* (1902).
Galerie Bernheim-Jeune, Paris. *Exposition d'oeuvres nouvelles par Bonnard, Denis, Maillol, Roussel, Vallotton, and Vuillard* (May 1902).
Galerie Bernheim-Jeune, Paris. *Tapisseries d'Aristide Maillol* (January-February 1911).
Galerie Alfred Flechtheim, Berlin. *Maillol* (1928). Essay by Count Kessler.
Exposition des Beaux-Arts et de la Gazette des Beaux-Arts, Paris. *Gauguin, ses amis, L'école de Pont Aven, et l'académie Julian* (1934). Preface by Maurice Denis, "L'Epoque du symbolism." Catalogue by Raymond Escholier.
Galerie Charpentier, Paris. *Georges de Monfreid et son ami, Gauguin.* (1938). Preface by Maurice Denis.
Stedelijk Museum, Amsterdam. *French Sculpture* (1939).
Galerie Parvillé, Paris. *L'Ecole de Pont-Aven et les Nabis: 1888-89* (1943). Preface by Maurice Denis.
Museum of Modern Art, New York. *Modern Painters and Sculptors as Illustrators* (1944). Catalogue by Monroe Wheeler.
Statens Museum fur Kunst, Copenhagen. *Maillol* (1947).
Galerie Charpentier, Paris. *Maillol* (1947). Preface by Jules Romains.
Blanch's Konstgalleri, Stockholm. *A. Maillol* (1947).
Kunsthalle, Bern. *Die Maler der Revue Blanche: Toulouse Lautrec und die Nabis* (1951). Catalogue by Fritz Hermann.
Musée National d'Art Moderne, Paris. *Bonnard, Vuillard, et les Nabis* (1955).
Musée des Augustins, Toulouse. *Achille Laugé et ses amis Maillol et Bourdelle* (1961). Essay by Charles Pornon.
Galerie Daber, Paris. *Maillol* (1961).
Musée National d'Art Moderne, Paris. *Hommage à Maillol* (1961). Preface by Jean Cassou.
Hamburg, Amsterdam, Frankfurt, Stuttgart, Munich, Dortmund. *Aristide Maillol* (1961-62). Preface by Alfred Hentzen.
Musée National d'Art Moderne, Paris. *Les Sources du XXe siècle—Les Arts en Europe de 1884 à 1914.* Translated as *Gateway to the Twentieth Century: Art and Culture in a Changing World.* New York, 1962.
Galerie Pierre, Stockholm. *Maillol* (1962).
Minneapolis Institute of Arts, Minneapolis, Minn. *The Nabis and Their Circle* (1962).
Kunsthalle, Mannheim. *Die Nabis und Ihre Freunde* (1963-64). Preface by Heinz Fuchs.
Musée des Beaux-Arts, Neuchâtel. *Maillol* (1964).
Yale University Art Gallery, New Haven, Conn. *Neo-Impressionists and Nabis in the Collection of Arthur G. Altschul* (1965). Edited by Robert Herbert.
Tate Gallery, London. *Gauguin and the Pont-Aven Group* (1966). Arts Council of Great Britain.
Grand Palais, Paris. *Les Indépendants à la belle époque: 1895-1901* (1966). Société des Artistes Indépendants.
Palais des Beaux-Arts, Lille. *Emile Bernard* (1967).
Musée des Beaux-Arts, Angers. *Maurice Denis et les Nabis* (1967).

Orangerie, Paris. *Vuillard—Roussel* (1968). Catalogue written by Pierre Georgel.

Art Gallery of Ontario, Toronto. *The Sacred and Profane in Symbolist Art* (1969). Catalogue directed by Luigi Carluccio.

Perls Gallery, New York. *Aristide Maillol* (1970).

Orangerie des Tuileries, Paris. *Maurice Denis* (1970). Preface by Louis Hautecoeur. Catalogue by Anne Dayez.

Palais des Arts et de la Culture, Brest. *Maillol; sculptures, dessins* (1971).

Art Gallery of Ontario. *E. Vuillard* (1971). Written by John Russell.

Perls Gallery, New York. *Maillol* (1972).

Hayward Gallery, London. *French Symbolist Painters* (1972). Arts Council of Great Britain.

Hayward Gallery, London. *Pioneers of Modern Sculpture* (1973). Arts Council of Great Britain. Essay by Albert E. Elsen.

Grand Palais, Paris. *Chefs-d'oeuvres de la Tapisserie du XIVe au XVIe siècles* (1973-74). Catalogue by Geneviève Souchal.

Solomon R. Guggenheim Museum, New York. *Aristide Maillol: 1861-1944* (1975-76). Essay by John Rewald, "Maillol Remembered."

Art Gallery of Ontario, Toronto, Canada. *Puvis de Chavannes and the Modern Tradition* (1975). Catalogue by Richard J. Wattenmaker.

Cleveland Museum of Art, Cleveland, Ohio. *Japonisme: Japanese Influence on French Art, 1854-1910* (1975). Essays by Gabriel Weisberg, Gerald Needham, et al.

Contemporary Sculpture Center, Tokyo, Osaka. *Aristide Maillol* (1976).

Staatliche Kunsthalle, Baden-Baden. *Maillol* (1978). Catalogue and preface by Hans Albert Peters, texts by John Rewald, et al.

Musée Hyacinthe Rigaud, Perpignan, France. *Maillol au Palais des Rois de Majorque* (1979). Essays by John Rewald and Marie-Claude Valaison.

Centre Cultural de la Caixa de Pensions, Barcelona. *Maillol: 1861-1944* (1979). Essays by Maria Lluisa Borras, et al.

Royal Academy of Arts, London. *Post-Impressionism: Cross-Currents in European Painting* (1979-80). Introduction by Alan Bowness, essays by John House, Mary Anne Stevens, et. al.

Index

Vallotton, Félix
  Bathers, 63
Van Gogh, Vincent, 17, 18, 22, 26, 33
Venus, 43, 64
Vehbi, Sunbul-Záde, 77
Verkade, Jan, 52
  La Vie seigneurial, 57, 58
  The Bath, 57
  Embroidery, 57
Vierny, Mme. Dina, 1, 88, 91, 94, 95

Villeneuve-St. Georges, 14, 15, 75
Virgin Mary, 58, 64
Vollard, Ambrose, 14, 15, 75, 80
Vuillard, Edouard, 14, 17, 21, 43, 46, 59, 64

Waldemar-George, 4
Watteau, Antoine, 65
Wattenmaker, Richard, 23

Yvon, Adolphe, 10